WORLD CUP 2002

FOOTBALL SUPERSTARS OF THE

WORLD CUP
2002

Tim Hill

This is a Parragon Book
First published in 2002

Parragon, Queen Street House, 4 Queen Street, Bath BA1 1HE, UK.

Copyright ©Parragon 2002
All Photographs copyright Getty Images

ISBN Hardback: 0 75257 906 1
ISBN Paperback: 0 75257 907 X

Conceived, designed and produced by
Atlantic Publishing, London

Acknowledgments
This book would not have been possible without the help of
Rick Mayston and Matt Stevens

Thanks also to Steve Torrington, Dave Sheppard, Brian Jackson, Alan Pinnock,
Peter Wright, Trevor Bunting, Simon Taylor, Sheila Harding, Christine Hoy, Maureen Hill,
Anthony Linden, Carol and Cliff Salter, Tom and Harry Nettleton.

Designed by: John Dunne
Pre press by Croxsons
Printed in Dubai

The 32 Teams in the World Cup Finals 2002

 Argentina

 Belgium

 Brazil

 Cameroon

 China

 Costa Rica

 Croatia

 Denmark

 Ecuador

 England

 France

 Germany

 Ireland

 Italy

 Japan

 Mexico

 Nigeria

 Paraguay

 Poland

 Portugal

 Russia

 Saudia Arabia

 Senegal

 Slovenia

 South Africa

 South Korea

 Spain

 Sweden

 Tunisia

 Turkey

 United States

 Uruguay

Contents

Introduction

David Beckham versus Diego Simeone, Michael Owen versus the entire Argentina defence, Sven-Goran Eriksson versus Sweden: these are just some of the mouthwatering prospects in store as the greatest footballing show on earth rolls into Japan and Korea this summer.

Fans from all corners of the globe will be adjusting their blinkers and talking up their country's chances. In World Cup year there is always the hope that your team will peak to perfection, while the other 31 contenders fall by the wayside.

For many it will be a triumph of hope over expectation. In reality, the likes of China, Senegal and Costa Rica might regard reaching the second round as a major achievement. On the other hand, it would be deemed a national disaster if tournament favourites France and Argentina failed at the first hurdle.

Despite finding themselves in this year's "Group of Death" and seeded outside the top eight, Eriksson's England side will go into the competition with a huge weight of expectation on their shoulders. Last September's stunning 5-1 win over Germany in Munich made sure of that. Mick McCarthy's resilient Republic of Ireland team, led by the inspirational Roy Keane, will also fancy their chances of reaching the knockout stage again.

Brazil remain one of the favourites, despite struggling through in third place in South America's qualifying group, behind Argentina and Ecuador. The four-time winners suffered a string of defeats against some of the lesser lights of international football. It was a pattern that has repeated itself all over the world in recent years, and the reason is simple. The so-called minnows are closing the gap all the time; no country is easy meat any more; all are capable of springing a surprise.

This book doesn't attempt to predict where the shocks will be. Nor does it suggest who might lift the trophy on June 30. But it does give an in-depth analysis of each country, and the players who will be making the headlines. It is an indispensable fans guide to what promises to be the most open and exciting World Cup ever.

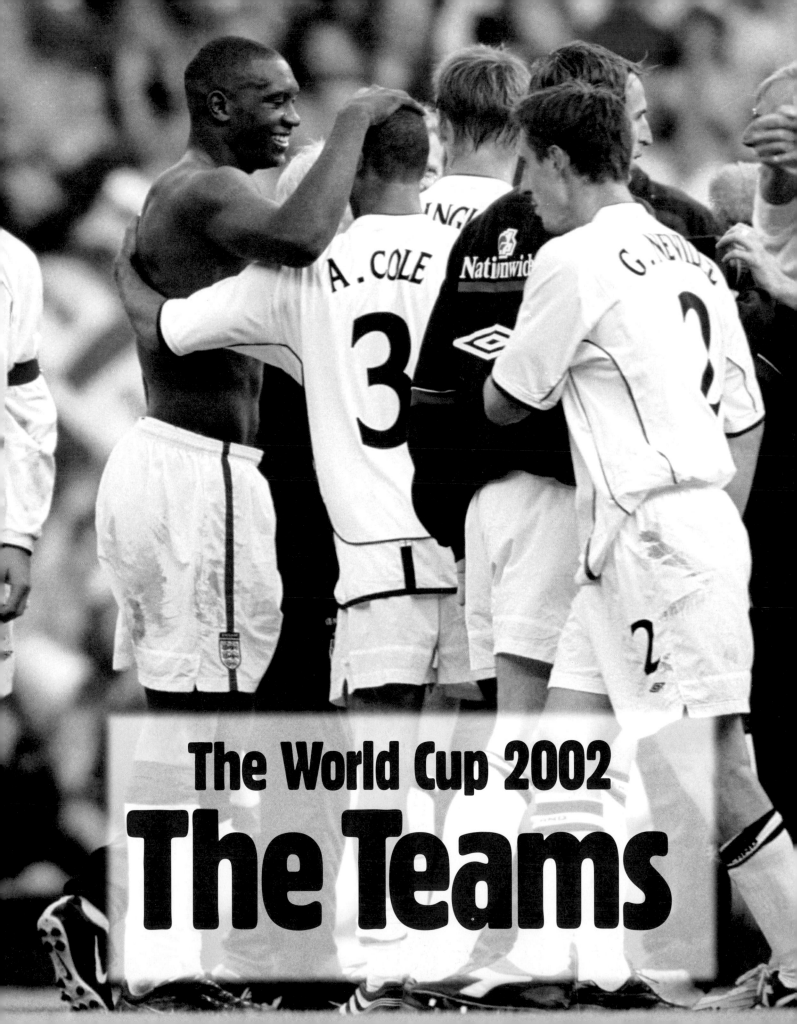

The World Cup 2002
The Teams

Argentina

Most pundits looking objectively at the World Cup finals think that the winners will come from the top South American side and Europe's best: Argentina and France. As holders, France have not had to show their class in a qualifying campaign. Argentina have and how. The team won 13, drew 4 and lost just once on their way to a 13th appearance in the finals. The only hiccup came in their away match against Brazil. When the competition reached its climax, however, it was the Brazilians who were sweating on results, while Argentina qualified with plenty to spare. Colombia, who themselves have a World Cup pedigree, were one of the sides to suffer badly at Argentina's hands. The Colombians lost 3-1 at home and 3-0 away, after which their coach Francisco Maturana was prompted to remark: "Its hell playing against Argentina". One of the few people who relished the fact that Argentina were drawn in England's group was David Beckham. Beckham's petulant spat with Diego Simeone four

The Finals

Group F
v Nigeria
v England
v Sweden

years ago left England to battle for more than an hour with 10 men. The fans have spent four years pondering what might have happened had Beckham stayed on the pitch. When he leads England out against Argentina on June 7, Beckham will have the chance to lay to rest the ghost of France '98, and it can't come soon enough for him. One difference this time round will be that Beckham and the rest of the Manchester United contingent will be facing one of their team-mates. Beckham versus Juan Sebastian Veron will give the match added spice, though Argentina have stars throughout the side. Claudio Lopez, Hernan Crespo and Gabriel Batistuta give Argentina one of the most potent attacks in world football. Defensively, England will have to be at their very best on June 7; if they aren't, Beckham and Owen's efforts in the attacking third could all be in vain.

Ariel Ortega of Argentina holds off the challenge from Jorge Huaman of Peru. Argentina won the match 2 - 0.

Path to the Finals

Argentina 4 Chile 1
Venezuela 0 Argentina 4
Argentina 1 Bolivia 0
Colombia 1 Argentina 3
Argentina 2 Ecuador 0
Brazil 3 Argentina 1
Argentina 1 Paraguay 1
Peru 1 Argentina 2
Argentina 2 Uruguay 1
Chile 0 Argentina 2
Argentina 5 Venezuela 0
Bolivia 3 Argentina 3
Argentina 3 Colombia 0
Ecuador 0 Argentina 2
Argentina 2 Brazil 1
Paraguay 2 Argentina 2
Argentina 2 Peru 0
Uruguay 1 Argentina 1

Argentina

Juan Veron and Gabriel Batistuta prepare for kick-off in the World Cup quarter-final match against Holland. Argentina lost 2-1.

Brazil

In many ways, Brazil encapsulates the spirit of the World Cup. It is the only country to have appeared in every tournament since 1930, and has won the trophy on a record four occasions. More often than not, Brazil has won in a style befitting the beautiful game. The team of 1970, which included Pele and Jairzinho, is regarded as the greatest ever.

The country suffered a huge disappointment in Spain 1982, when an all-star team led by Socrates went out to eventual winners Italy. It showed that the best team didn't always come out on top, and Brazilian sides since have tempered marvellous individual skills with gritty tournament play.

Current coach Luis Felipe Scolari likes his teams to have a steely quality about them. Not that it did Brazil much good in the qualifying series. Scolari's men squeezed into the last of

The Finals
Group C
v Turkey
v China
v Costa Rica

the four automatic qualifying places, having experienced a number of wobbles along the way. These included defeats in Paraguay and Ecuador who both finished above Brazil in the final table and also away to Chile, the group's wooden spoonists.

Brazil just managed to avoid the indignity of having to go through the play-offs. However, their status as the world's number one footballing nation has gone temporarily, at least. France replaced Brazil in FIFA's rankings just before Christmas.

Despite a less than impressive qualifying campaign, Brazil will still be among the favourites to go all the way this summer. Many of the stars of 1998 are still there, including Ronaldo, Roberto Carlos and Cafu. There is also the burgeoning talent of the younger stars, such as Lucio and Ronaldhinho. All will be burning with desire to make amends for Brazil's woeful performance in the final four years ago.

Rivaldo of Brazil and Magallanes of Uruguay in action in the Centenario Stadium, Montevideo.

Path to the Finals

Colombia 0 Brazil 0
Brazil 3 Ecuador 2
Peru 0 Brazil 1
Brazil 1 Uruguay 1
Paraguay 2 Brazil 1
Brazil 3 Argentina 1
Chile 3 Brazil 0
Brazil 5 Bolivia 0
Venezuela 0 Brazil 6
Brazil 1 Colombia 0
Ecuador 1 Brazil 0
Brazil 1 Peru 1
Uruguay 1 Brazil 0
Brazil 2 Paraguay 0
Argentina 2 Brazil 1
Brazil 2 Chile 0
Bolivia 3 Brazil 1
Brazil 3 Venezuela 0

Brazil

Brazil's Flavio Conceicao challenges Claudio Nunez of Chile during the Copa America match in Paraguay

Brazil

Bixente Lizarazu of France and Leandro of Brazil during the FIFA Confederations Cup semi-final match played in Korea.

Belgium

Belgium has an excellent record as far as reaching the World Cup finals is concerned. You have to go back to Argentina in 1978 to find a tournament for which the Belgians failed to qualify. And in the 1980s in particular, Belgium had a fine team. Runners-up to Germany in the 1980 European Championship, Belgium went on to top a group including Argentina at the 1982 World Cup, before flopping in the second round. At Mexico '86, Belgium finished behind Mexico and Paraguay in their group, but went through as one of the best third-placed teams. After that piece of fortune, Belgium went all the way to the semi-finals. They beat the Soviet Union and Spain, before losing to Argentina in the last four. That remains the country's best ever performance in a World Cup.

Four years later, at Italia '90, it was England who ended their interest, in the second round. A sweetly-struck volley by David Platt was the only goal of the game. 1994 saw Belgium once again go through as one of the best third-placed sides, before going down to Germany 3-2 in the second phase. It was 3rd place once again at the last World Cup. That was not to be enough to put them through this time, for an expanded 32-team tournament means that only the top two now progress.

The Finals

Group H
v Japan
v Tunisia
v Russia

Just three points separated Croatia, Belgium and Scotland at the end of their qualifying campaign for this summer's tournament. Belgium finished a point behind Croatia and had to face the Czech Republic in the play-offs. They came through that test, against many people's expectations.

Many of Belgians players are dotted around the leagues of Europe. Veteran midfielder Marc Wilmots, an important cog in the side, plays for Bundesliga side Schalke 04. Striker Emile Mpenza plays for the same club, though he is struggling with a long-term injury. One of the team's most exciting young players is 23-year-old striker Wesley Sonck, of Racing Genk. He is one of the few squad members who still play their club football in Belgium.

With Japan as the seeded opponents in group H, Belgium will be well fancied to make it to the second round, along with either Russia or Tunisia.

Path to the Finals

Belgium 0 Croatia 0
Latvia 0 Belgium 4
Belgium 10 San Marino 1
Scotland 2 Belgium 2
Belgium 3 Latvia 1
San Marino 1 Belgium 4
Belgium 2 Scotland 0
Croatia 1 Belgium 0

Scotland's Don Hutchinson breaks away from Glen De Boeck in the Qualifying match between Belgium and Scotland at King Baudouin Stadium, Brussels.

Cameroon

Cameroon can no longer be regarded as the entertaining new kids on the block. This summer marks their fifth appearance out of the last six World Cups, making the country the most successful from the African continent.

England fans will remember Cameroon's best performance to date. The two sides clashed at the quarter-final stage of Italia '90, and England needed two penalties to squeeze through 3-2. Earlier in the tournament, the Indomitable Lions had beaten reigning champions Argentina, with Romania and Colombia other notable scalps.

Cameroon finished bottom of their group in 1994 and 1998, Nigeria outperforming them on both occasions. More recently, things have taken a turn for the better. Cameroon won the African Nations Cup in 2000, something they haven't managed since 1988. The Indomitable Lions took the Olympic title in Sydney in the same year, beating a very talented Under-23 Spanish side on penalties in the final.

Cameroon's latest star and the man who found the net four times in that gold medal-winning performance in Australia is Patrick Mboma. The current African Footballer of the Year, Mboma was a journeyman player in France and Japan before Cagliari gave him his chance in Serie A. He went on a hot scoring streak with one of the lesser lights of Italian football. When Parma sold Hernan Crespo to Lazio for £37 million, the club replaced him with Mboma for a fraction of the money.

Cameroon's official FIFA ranking puts them behind Germany, Saudi Arabia and the Republic of Ireland. The bookmakers have been more canny, placing Cameroon second behind Germany in Group E. And as everybody knows, the bookmakers don't get it wrong too often.

The Finals

Group E
v Ireland
v Saudi Arabia
v Germany

Villarroel of Chile challenges Cameroon's Joseph Job during the 1998 World Cup group B game in Nantes, France.

Path to the Finals

Libya 0 Cameroon 3
Cameroon 3 Angola 0
Togo 0 Cameroon 2
Cameroon 1 Zambia 0
Cameroon 1 Libya 0
Angola 2 Cameroon 0
Cameroon 2 Togo 0
Zambia 2 Cameroon 2

China

China's qualification for their first-ever World Cup finals has thrown up a fact which will undoubtedly crop up again and again in sports quizzes. Their highly-regarded coach Bora Milutinovic made it five World Cups in a row when he steered China to the finals. Remarkably, he has led a different country to each World Cup since 1986: Mexico, Costa Rica, USA, Nigeria and now China.

China profited from the innovation of having co-hosts for this year's tournament. Japan and South Korea are two of the strongest sides in Asia, and the fact that they didn't have to qualify was a distinct advantage to the other contenders from that region.

China eased through a group which included Oman, Uzbekistan, Qatar and the United Arab Emirates. Five wins and a draw in the first six games meant that qualification was secured with two games to spare.

The Finals

Group C
v Costa Rica
v Brazil
v Turkey

Crystal Palace fans in particular will be familiar with two of China's top players, Fan Zhiyi and Sun Jihai. Fan became a great favourite with the Eagles, though he has now moved on to Dundee United. Sun found it more difficult to settle and returned home. He is currently attracting a lot of interest from Serie A clubs AC Milan and Torino.

The all-round quality of China's squad isn't likely to be high enough for the country to cause too many upsets this time round. But with a vast population and huge interest in the game, this could be the last World Cup in which China are regarded as no-hopers.

Path to the Finals

China 3 UAE 0
Oman 0 China 2
Qatar 1 China 1
China 2 Uzbekistan 0
UAE 0 China 1
China 1 Oman 0
China 3 Qatar 0
Uzbekistan 1 China 0
China 10 Maldives 1
Maldives 0 China 1
Cambodia 0 China 4
China 5 Indonesia 1
China 3 Cambodia 1
Indonesia 0 China 2

China celebrate Hao Haidong's goal during the match against between Qatar. China won the game 3 - 0.

Costa Rica

After missing out on the last two World Cups, Costa Rica now has the chance to build on the impressive debut the country made on the international stage at Italia '90. Twelve years ago, the newcomers from the CONCACAF region found themselves up against Brazil and two tough European opponents in Scotland and Sweden. The team stunned the Tartan Army by beating Scotland 1-0, went down to Brazil by the same score, then showed that the opening game was no fluke by winning 2-1 against Sweden. It was enough to take them to the second phase. The team lost 4-1 to Czechoslovakia, but it was still a fine achievement to reach the second round at the very first attempt.

This time round, Costa Rica comfortably topped the group which covers North and Central America, along with the Caribbean. The USA and Mexico had to settle for qualification via the minor placings, while Jamaica another team with a World Cup pedigree was well off the pace.

Most of the Costa Rica players will be unknown quantities to England fans with the notable exception of Paulo Wanchope. The leggy, unpredictable striker made a name for himself at Derby, struggled for form at West Ham, and is now helping fire Manchester City to an immediate return to the Premiership. For Costa Rica, Wanchope operates in tandem with Rolando Fonseca, and the pair provide the cutting edge in a fast, counter-attacking side which tends to play a 3-5-2 system.

With Brazil once again the seeded team in their group, the Costa Ricans will surely be vying with China and Turkey for the second qualification spot. It's a tall order, though no more difficult than the task faced by the country 12 years ago in Italy.

The Finals

Group C
v China
v Turkey
v Brazil

Reynaldo Parks of Costa Rica in action during the World Cup Qualifier against Mexico played in Costa Rica.

Path to the Finals

Costa Rica 2 Honduras 2
Costa Rica 3 Trinidad & Tobago 0
United States 1 Costa Rica 0
Mexico 1 Costa Rica 2
Costa Rica 2 Jamaica 1
Honduras 2 Costa Rica 3
Trinidad & Tobago 0 Costa Rica 2
Costa Rica 2 United States 0
Costa Rica 0 Mexico 0
Jamaica 0 Costa Rica 1

Croatia

Croatia has achieved a great deal in the 12 years since the country returned to world football as a separate nation. For the previous half-century, Croatia had been subsumed within Yugoslavia, both on the political and the sporting fronts. The signs of a fine side were there for all to see at Euro '96. Top quality players such as Zvonimir Boban, Robert Prosinecki and Alen Boksic helped Croatia reach the quarter-finals in style. An indisciplined performance against Germany at that stage cost them dear, and they lost 2-1.

At France '98, Croatia avenged that defeat by routing Germany 3-0, also at the quarter-final stage. The team then went down 2-1 to France in the semis. A victory by the same margin over Holland in the play-off for third place meant Croatia had come from nowhere to the third best team in the world in just eight years.

Two years later, Croatia didn't even make it to the European Championships in Holland and Belgium. One of the chief reasons for the rapid decline was that the nucleus of their superb side was a crop of ageing players. A string of poor results following the heady days of France '98 saw Croatia drop to 19 in FIFA's world rankings. The qualifying campaign for this year's World Cup was more encouraging. Latvia and San Marino didn't provide much of a test, and the group came down to a three-horse race between Croatia, Belgium and Scotland. The latter two suffered one defeat each, while Croatia remained unbeaten, and that was the difference as just three points separated the countries in the final table.

While the team was strong enough to win their qualifying group, it is going to be very tough for Croatia to repeat the success of four years ago. There are some new faces in the squad, but the class still comes from the veterans. Prosinecki has been a class apart for Division I side Portsmouth this season. Boksic who missed France '98 through injury is brilliant on the ball for Middlesbrough, though his work rate when the opposition are in possession is less impressive. Davor Suker, who won the Golden Boot with six goals at the last World Cup, is currently without a club. If players such as these can stay fit and gather themselves for one last hurrah, then Croatia could make an impact. At the very least, they will fancy themselves to get the better of Ecuador and Mexico and progress to the second round along with Italy.

Path to the Finals

Belgium 0 Croatia 0
Croatia 1 Scotland 1
Croatia 4 Latvia 1
Croatia 4 San Marino 0
Latvia 0 Croatia 1
Scotland 0 Croatia 0
San Marino 0 Croatia 4
Croatia 1 Belgium 0

Croatia's Stjepan Tomas and Robert Kovac battle with Don Hutchison of Scotland at Hampden Park in Glasgow. The game ended in a 0-0 draw

Denmark

Denmark is another country whose form has ebbed and flowed in recent years. The Danes failed to qualify for the European Championship in 1992, then were given a last-minute entry into the tournament after war-torn Yugoslavia withdrew. Denmark went on to win the competition, beating Germany in the final. They failed to reach USA '94, but made it to the quarter-finals four years later. At the group stage of France '98, the Danes lost only to the host nation, with whom they qualified. They then enjoyed a magnificent 4-1 win over Nigeria in the second round, but were edged out by Brazil in a five-goal thriller in the last eight, with Rivaldo on target twice for the South Americans. It meant that Denmark had only lost by the odd goal to the two favourites and the teams that went on to contest the final. Denmark again came up against France at Euro 2000. It wasn't so close this time. The game ended 3-0 to the world champions, and the Danes lost by the same score to

The Finals
Group A
v France
v Uruguay
v Senegal

Holland. A 2-0 defeat by the Czech Republic completed a miserable tournament.

Qualification for this year's World Cup has offered Danish fans more encouragement. They went through the 10-match series unbeaten, and with Bulgaria and the Czech Republic in their group, that was no mean achievement.

The team includes Everton's Thomas Gravesen and Sunderland 'keeper Thomas Sorensen. England fans will also remember Jon Dahl Tomasson, who didn't show his best during his time at Newcastle United, but is performing well for both Feyenoord and the national team. Tomasson forms a strike duo with Ebbe Sand, who plays for Bundesliga side Schalke 04. Sand hit 22 goals last season to make him the top striker in Germany's top league.

For the third major tournament running, the Danes find themselves up against France at the group stage. It is hard to envisage anything other than a victory for the champions and favourites. The other teams look more beatable. Uruguay only scraped through the play-offs after finishing fifth in the South America group, while Senegal are the outsiders and lowest-ranked team of the 32 finalists. Another appearance in the knockout stages looks a distinct possibility for the Danes.

Tofting of Denmark tussles with Kevin Horlock of Northern Ireland at Windsor Park in Belfast.

Path to the Finals

Iceland 1 Denmark 2
Northern Ireland 1 Denmark 1
Denmark 1 Bulgaria 1
Malta 0 Denmark 0
Czech Republic 0 Denmark 0
Denmark 2 Czech Republic 1
Denmark 2 Malta 1
Denmark 1 Northern Ireland 1
Bulgaria 0 Denmark 2
Denmark 6 Iceland 0

Ecuador

Ecuador made it to their first World Cup in fine style. They finished second behind the runaway winners Argentina in the South America group. Some impressive names in world football found themselves looking up at Ecuador in the final group table. These included Uruguay, Peru, Colombia, Chile and even mighty Brazil.

Ecuador's strength lay in a fortress-like home record. In the rarefied atmosphere of Quito, high in the Andes, Ecuador won six, drew two and lost just once to Argentina.

Ecuador's hero on the glory road to Japan and Korea was striker Augustin Delgado. He hit nine goals in 16 games to take Ecuador to the brink of qualification. One of those strikes was dubbed the most important goal in Ecuador's history: the one which gave the country an historic 1-0 home win over Brazil.

The Finals
Group G
v Italy

v Mexico

v Croatia

Delgado didn't hit the goal which clinched World Cup qualification, however. That honour went to team-mate Jaime Kaviedes, in a 1-1 draw against Uruguay. They had made history with a game against last placed Chile to spare.

Delgado finished the qualifying series as joint-top scorer with Argentina's highly-rated Hernan Crespo. That was enough to get the phones ringing, and it was Southampton's Gordon Strachan who stole a march on the other interested parties by signing him for the Premiership club. Strachan paid just £3.5 million for Delgado; Crespo would sell for many times that figure.

Ecuador will come down to earth quite literally in the World Cup. The altitude advantage they enjoyed in Quito won't be there when they take on Italy, Croatia and Mexico. How well their form holds up as they take to the road will be the key factor for the South American debutants.

Path to the Finals

Ecuador 2 Venezuela 0

Brazil 3 Ecuador 2

Paraguay 3 Ecuador 1

Ecuador 2 Peru 1

Argentina 2 Ecuador 0

Ecuador 0 Colombia 0

Ecuador 2 Bolivia 0

Uruguay 4 Ecuador 0

Ecuador 1 Chile 0

Venezuela 1 Ecuador 2

Ecuador 1 Brazil 0

Ecuador 2 Paraguay 1

Peru 1 Ecuador 2

Ecuador 0 Argentina 2

Colombia 0 Ecuador 0

Bolivia 1 Ecuador 5

Ecuador 1 Uruguay 1

Chile 0 Ecuador 0

Raul Guerrou in action during the World Cup Qualifier against Brazil. Ecuador won the match 1 - 0.

England

By the time the World Cup gets under way, most England fans will have convinced themselves that the title is there for the taking. Using the tried and trusted selective memory technique, they will point out that a 10-man team came within an ace of beating Argentina four years ago; and that Sven-Goran Eriksson's men looked world beaters in the 5-1 demolition job on Germany last September. The failure at Euro 2000 and the unimpressive performances against Holland, Greece and Sweden over the past year will all be studiously overlooked.

David Beckham and Michael Owen are undoubtedly the two key players in the squad. Both were there in France four years ago as burgeoning talents; now they are both truly world-class. Steven Gerrard and Paul Scholes are the other two who can lay claim to joining the elite. Should all four be on top of their game in the World Cup, England will be a potent attacking force. Defensively, it all looks still to play for. Rio Ferdinand, Wes Brown and Sol Campbell have all looked shaky on occasions; Ashley Cole is exciting going forward, less secure at the back; Gary Neville, Danny Mills and Jamie Carragher may well find themselves vying for the right-back spot. A settled defensive unit will be vital for success, and the time for experimenting is fast running out.

Not being among the eight seeded teams hit England hard in the draw. The pecking order for the seeding process was based on performances in the last three World Cups, together with current FIFA rankings. Reaching the semi-finals of Italia '90, and the second round in 1998 helped England's cause; but

The Finals

Group F
v Sweden
v Argentina
v Nigeria

Sheringham and Beckham celebrate qualification.

England

failure to qualify for USA 94 was the critical factor.

Even allowing for the fact that England were relegated to the group of second-ranks teams, the draw could still have been kinder. Argentina romped through the South America group during qualifying; Nigeria is one of the strongest African sides, and matched England's World Cup performance four years ago; and it is more than 30 years since England recorded a victory over Sweden. There was no other contender for this summer's "Group of Death".

Eriksson was his usual phlegmatic self when the draw was made. There was a shrug of the shoulders, and a quiet determination to get on with the job. The message was clear: it was a tough draw for England - but it was a tough draw for Argentina, Sweden and Nigeria, too.

The result against Argentina - England's second opponents - may not be crucial this summer, but the history

Top right: Captain Beckham takes time out on the training field. Above: England's victorious qualifiers - Back row, Campbell, Heskey, Ferdinand, Seaman and Owen. Front row, Barmby, Gerrard, Scholes, Neville, Beckham and Cole.

England

Path to the Finals

England 0 Germany 1
Finland 0 England 0
England 2 Finland 1
Albania 1 England 3
Greece 0 England 3
Germany 1 England 5
England 2 Albania 0
England 2 Greece 2

Owen celebrates during the historic 5-1 victory over Germany.

England

between the two countries will guarantee the match a massive build-up. England came out on top in an ugly quarter-final encounter in 1966. In 1986, Maradona's two goals one scored with his hand, the other with his quicksilver feet won another quarter-final battle for Argentina. And in France four years ago, there was Owen's stunning strike, Beckham's red card, Campbell's disallowed goal and Batty's penalty shoot-out agony.

Depending on how the other groups pan out, England could face both France and Brazil in the following rounds, should they win through from Group F. The difficulty of the path mapped out for England at the draw gave rise to one incontestable observation: if England are going to win, they are going to have to do it the hard way.

Top right: Scholes, Fowler and Beckham. Above: Beckham lines up England's defensive wall as Ferdinand looks on.

England

Top left: Owen jumps for joy as the rout of Germany is complete.

Top right: Eriksson celebrates his team's success. His message about England's draw for the finals was clear: it was a tough draw for England but it was a tough draw for Argentina, Sweden and Nigeria, too.

Above: England celebrate qualification after Beckham's wonder strike.

Opposite: Beckham scoring from one of his sensational free kicks in Greece.

England

England

 England

France

Anyone who looks with a concerned eye at the strength of the French squad has to grab any crumb of comfort going. One of those might be the recent form of Fabien Barthez, one of the stars of the side which won the tournament four years ago. Another might be a vague hope that Les Bleus will be ring-rusty, having missed out on the rigours of a qualifying campaign.

In reality, there are few straws to clutch at, and the top-ranked side in the world will present a huge obstacle to the aspirations of the other 31 countries taking part. With full-backs Lilian Thuram and Bixente Lizarazu raiding down the flanks, adding to the awesome midfield creativity and strike power, it will take a good side to expose any goalkeeping errors that Barthez might make.

Ironically, it was France's rock solid defence which provided the platform for their success four years ago. The perceived weakness then was up front. It was no surprise that each of the three goals that beat Brazil in the final came from midfielders, one from Emmanuel Petit and two from the outstanding Zinedine Zidane. The last four years has seen the emergence of Thierry Henry and David Trezeguet, two world-class strikers to add to an already potent side.

One player who won't be there for France this time is Didier Deschamps. He was famously described as a mere "water-carrier" by Eric Cantona. Patrick Vieira the man Deschamps kept out of the side gets through just as much midfield donkey work as the former captain, and arguably offers much more when he is in possession. Yet another reason to suggest that France will again be the team to beat this year.

If England emerge from their group in second place, they may well find themselves up against Les Bleus in the second round. Should that happen, it will either be the end of the road for Sven-Goran Eriksson's men, or the launchpad to send England all the way to the final.

The Finals

Group A
v Senegal
v Uruguay
v Denmark

Patrick Vieira (left) and Robert Pires (right) of France challenge Fabio (centre) of Brazil during the FIFA Confederations Cup semi-final played in Suwon, Korea. France won the game 2-1.
Opposite: World Cup winners in Paris 1998.

Path to the Finals

France qualified to the World Cup by winning the 1998 World Cup in Paris. They are the last winners to have this privilege.

🏳️ France

Germany

Anyone who writes off Germany's chances in a World Cup does so at their peril. The Germans may have needed a play-off victory over Ukraine to make it to the finals, but no country has a better record when it comes to peaking for big tournaments. With three victories, Germany still trails Brazil as far as winning the World Cup is concerned. But if the net is widened slightly to focus on teams which have reached at the last four, then Germany who have made it to the semis on nine occasions are the best in the business.

Germany's progress has been halted at the quarter-final stage at the last two World Cups almost a crisis by that country's skyhigh standards. If anyone doubted that the team was in a transitional phase, then a miserable first round exit at Euro 2000 confirmed it. England fans enjoyed rubbing salt into Germany's wounds with that stunning 5-1 result in Munich last September. It was two drawn games against Finland, however, which proved just as costly.

There have been signs that the sleeping giant may be about to wake up. Germany left Wembley with all three points in the qualifiers, thanks to a Dietmar Hamann strike; and the team eased through a potentially tricky tie against Shevchenko and Co. in the play-offs. England fans know all about the qualities of Ziege, Hamann and Babbel. In Oliver Kahn Germany has the world's top goalkeeper, and Michael Ballack's performances have made him one of the hottest properties in Europe. Even with players of this stature, Germany will still only be among a cluster of teams ranked behind France and Argentina as likely winners this summer. Having less pressure than usual on their shoulders could be a distinct advantage to Rudi Voller's men.

The Finals

Group E
v Saudi Arabia
v Ireland
v Cameroon

Path to the Finals

Germany 2 Greece 0
England 0 Germany 1
Germany 2 Albania 1
Greece 2 Germany 4
Finland 2 Germany 2
Albania 0 Germany 2
Germany 1 England 5
Germany 0 Finland 0

Play off
1st Leg
Ukraine 1 Germany 1
2nd Leg
Germany 4 Ukraine 1

Germany win
on aggregate 5-2

Germany celebrate qualification after the play-off second leg match against Ukraine. They won 4-1, qualifying for the World Cup with a 5-2 aggregate win.

Germany

Andrei Shevchenko of Ukraine runs at Jens Nowotny of Germany during the play-off second leg match in Dortmund.

Ireland

It could be said that Mick McCarthy's Republic of Ireland team has eclipsed the World Cup achievements of 1990 and 1994 even before a ball has been kicked. Jack Charlton's team of a decade ago had a core of class players from teams such as Liverpool and Manchester Utd. With the exception of Roy Keane, Mick McCarthy has had fewer top-drawer players at his disposal in recent years. If that weren't hardship enough, the Republic found themselves in a qualifying group with the superstars of Holland and Portugal.

The Republic matched Portugal's performance in the campaign. Both teams finished with seven wins and three draws in the 10-match series, with Portugal edging the

The Finals

Group E
v Cameroon
v Germany
v Saudi Arabia

Republic into second place on goal difference. It meant a play-off against Iran, but that was still a stunning success compared with Holland, who were left to go home, lick their wounds and plan for the European Championship in 2004.

The Republic lost their unbeaten record when they conceded in the last minute against Iran in Teheran. They had already done enough in the home leg, though, and the party began.

The Republic's strength as a well-organised, hard-working side which is very difficult to break down will be a huge advantage this summer. If the matches go to form, then they should be vying with Cameroon for the right to go through alongside the seeded team, Germany. The inconsistency that the Germans have shown over the past couple of years will give McCarthy even more room for optimism.

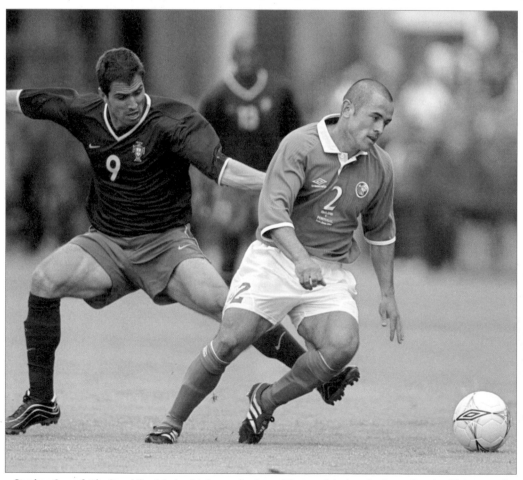

Stephen Carr of the Republic of Ireland takes on Pauleta of Portugal during the Group Two Qualifying match played at Lansdowne Road, Dublin.

Path to the Finals

Holland 2 Ireland 2
Portugal 1 Ireland 1
Ireland 2 Estonia 0
Cyprus 0 Ireland 4
Andorra 0 Ireland 3
Ireland 3 Andorra 1
Ireland 1 Portugal 1
Estonia 0 Ireland 2
Ireland 1 Holland 0
Ireland 4 Cyprus 0

Play off
1st Leg
Ireland 2 Iran 0
2nd Leg
Iran 1 Ireland 0

Ireland win
on aggregate 2-1

Ireland

Jason McAteer of the Republic of Ireland evades Phillip Cocu of Holland during the World Cup Qualifier played at Lansdowne Road in Dublin, Ireland. The Republic of Ireland won the game 1-0.

Ireland

Matt Holland of Republic of Ireland in action during the FIFA 2002 World Cup Qualifier against Holland played at Lansdowne Road

Ireland

The Republic of Ireland players celebrate victory after the World Cup Qualifier against Holland played at Lansdowne Road.

Italy

Italy are many people's favourites to be crowned champions this summer and equal Brazil's record of four tournament wins. All the indicators look good for the Azzurri. In the last two major tournaments France '98 and Euro 2000 Italy lost narrowly to France. FIFA's No. 1 team needed a penalty shoot-out to win their quarter-final against Italy four years ago. The two teams met in the final of Euro 2000, with a David Trezeguet Golden Goal deciding the outcome.

The Italians put aside these disappointments to qualify for Japan and Korea with six wins and two draws from their eight-match series. They conceded just three goals in 12 hours of football, underlining the defensive qualities for which the country has long been renowned. The regular back line consists of Alessandro Nesta, Fabio Cannavaro and Paolo Maldini. Thirty-three-year-old Maldini is playing as well as ever and would love to bow out of international football with a win in his fourth World Cup.

Further up the field, Italy has the creativity and firepower to trouble any team. Filippo Inzaghi, Christian Vieri and Alessandro del Piero give coach Giovanni Trapattoni attacking options that many countries would love to have. But Trapattoni has nominated the Roma playmaker Francesco Totti as his ace in the pack. He believes Totti can have the kind of influence that Zidane had in France's triumph four years ago.

The draw has favoured Italy. They will face Ecuador and Mexico at the group stage, along with a Croatia side which is unlikely to be as strong as four years ago. It's hard to see Italy failing to progress to the knockout stage, and they have the ammunition to go a long way in the tournament.

The Finals
Group G
v Ecuador
v Croatia
v Mexico

Path to the Finals

Hungary 2 Italy 2
Italy 3 Romania 0
Italy 2 Georgia 0
Romania 0 Italy 2
Italy 4 Lithuania 4
Georgia 1 Italy 2
Lithuania 0 Italy 0
Italy 1 Hungary 0

Filippo Inzaghi in action during Italy's match against Hungary. Italy won the game 1 - 0.

Italy

Paolo Maldini in the game against Hungary.

 Japan

Japan and Korea 2002 might be one of the last World Cups when countries breathe a sigh of relief at being drawn against Japan. Seeded for this summer's tournament as co-hosts, Japan is a nation on the up in world football. The formation of the J-League in 1993 was a landmark in the development of the game. Stars of the calibre of Gary Lineker and Brazil's captain Dunga were drafted in to provide glamour and quality. They were role models for Japanese youngsters, who took up the game in huge numbers. In 1994, just one year after the professional league had been established, Japan missed out on World Cup qualification by a whisker. A last-minute goal conceded in their final match against Iraq meant that there was no World Cup debut for the country in the USA. Japan finally made its first appearance in the finals at France '98. The team lost all three games, but it wasn't embarrassed. Both Argentina and a very strong Croatia side could only manage 1-0 victories over the Japanese. Despite finishing the last World Cup without a point, Japan did have a star performer in Hidetoshi Nakata. Nakata moved to Serie A shortly after France '98, and has starred for Roma in the past couple of seasons. An army of Japanese journalists follows his every move in Italy. Nakata's emergence as the superstar of Asian football means that young football fans in Japan don't have to look abroad for their heroes any more. Where Nakata has led, others are bound to follow. It won't be in time for this World Cup, though, and the best Japan can hope for is to take a few scalps along the way.

The Finals
Group H
v Belgium
v Russia
v Tunisia

Path to the Finals

Japan co-hosting with South Korea did not have to qualify for the World Cup.

Hidetoshi Nakata of Japan takes on the Brazil defence during the FIFA Confederations Cup match which ended in a 0 – 0 draw.

Mexico

Mexico is the traditional powerhouse of the CONCACAF region. 2002 will be the country's twelfth appearance in the finals, which they have hosted twice. It was the two occasions when Mexico played on home soil 1970 and 1986 that the country enjoyed its best run. In 1970, the team dropped just one point at the group stage, before going down 4-1 to Italy in the quarter-finals. Sixteen years later, Mexico again notched five points out of six in the first round. They went on to beat Bulgaria, and only went down 2-1 to Germany on penalties after 120 minutes of goalless football.

Mexico progressed to the knockout stage in 1994 and 1998. In the USA there was more penalty agony as they lost out to Bulgaria. At France '98, Germany was their nemesis again, though at least the result was determined in open play this time: it finished 2-1 to the Germans.

Getting to Japan and Korea was anything but straightforward for Mexico. With one game remaining they were lying in third place, behind Costa Rica and the USA. With only three teams to qualify, it wasn't a foregone conclusion, particularly as they were level on points with Honduras the team they were to meet in their final match. Mexico won the game in the Azteca Stadium, a result which nudged them ahead of the

The Finals
Group G
v Ecuador
v Croatia
v Mexico

USA in the final table. The unemphatic fashion in which Mexico claimed their World Cup place cost two coaches their jobs. Manuel Lapente was in charge at the start of the campaign. He resigned, and former international Enrique Menza took over. His reign ended when he became the first Mexico coach to lose a World Cup qualifier at home. Javier Aguirre came in and steadied the ship in the latter stages, and will take Mexico to the finals.

Mexico's star striker in the qualifiers, with nine goals, was Cuauhtemoc Blanco. He has threatened not to go to the World Cup, following a dispute over travel costs between Spain where plays his club football and Mexico during the qualifiers. All Mexico fans will be hoping the issue is resolved amicably. The team will need him if Mexico are going to cause an upset and make it to the second round. The FIFA rankings put them ahead of Croatia and Ecuador, though the bookmakers odds suggest that Mexico will be propping up the table when the group matches are over.

Path to the Finals

United States 2 Mexico 0
Mexico 4 Jamaica 0
Trinidad & Tobago 1 Mexico 1
Mexico 1 Costa Rica 2
Honduras 3 Mexico 1
Mexico 1 United States 0
Jamaica 1 Mexico 2
Mexico 3 Trinidad & Tobago 0
Costa Rica 0 Mexico 0
Mexico 3 Honduras 0

Mexican Goalkeeper Oswaldo Sanchez punches the ball away during the 2nd Round Qualifying match against Costa Rica.

Nigeria

It wasn't so very long ago when top European and South American sides would have relished the prospect of straight-forward victories against African teams. Not any longer. African football is stylish, exuberant and full of flair, and no longer suffers from the naivety of a few years ago.

Nigeria is one of the strongest countries in what is becoming a very competitive arena in world football. The Nigerians made their World Cup debut as recently USA '94, yet the signs of their emerging strength were already there. Between 1985 and 1993 Nigeria reached the final of the world Under-17 championship four times, winning it twice. The side which won in 1993 included Nwankwo Kanu and Celestine Babayaro, now big-time players with Arsenal and Chelsea respectively.

At USA '94 Nigeria topped a group including Argentina,

The Finals
Group F
v Argentina
v Sweden
v England

Bulgaria and Greece. They came within a minute of beating Italy in the second round before succumbing by the odd goal in extra-time. Their performances surprised many who weren't aware of the platform that had been built at junior level.

Four years later, in France, the Nigerians were a known quantity and a perceived threat, yet Spain, Paraguay and Bulgaria still finished behind them at the group stage. Once again, they went out in the second round, this time to Denmark.

By then just about all of Nigeria's internationals were playing their football abroad. Many of the top club sides in Europe recognised the quality of players such as Finidi George and Taribo West, and in their turn, the players improved even more by turning out regularly in leagues such as Serie A and the Premiership.

Nigeria's present squad includes several players from France '98, and one or two from USA '94. The Super Eagles, as the side is known, will thus be vastly experienced, as well as full of flair. They respect no reputations, fear no one. Nigeria has already taken a number of World Cup scalps and will be out to take a few more this summer.

Nwankwo Kanu jumps on Victor Agali s back after his team-mate scores during the World Cup 2002 Group B Second Round Qualifying match against Liberia.

Path to the Finals

Nigeria 2 Sierra Leone 0
Liberia 2 Nigeria 1
Sierra Leone 0 Nigeria 5
Nigeria 3 Sudan 0
Ghana 0 Nigeria 0
Sierra Leone 1 Nigeria 0
Nigeria 2 Liberia 0
Sudan 0 Nigeria 4
Nigeria 3 Ghana 0

Paraguay

Paraguay had already featured in four World Cup finals when they went to France '98. They had even made the second round before in 1986, when England beat them 3-0. But it was Paraguay's performances in the last World Cup which really enhanced the reputation of this small country with a population of under 5 million.

They were inspired by their idiosyncratic goalkeeper Jose Luis Chilavert, who fancies himself as a dead-ball specialist as well as a shot-stopper. After creditable goalless draws against Bulgaria and Spain, Paraguay found themselves in the fortunate position of taking on a Nigeria side which had already qualified. Paraguay ran out 3-1 winners to set up a second round clash with France. It took a Golden Goal from Laurent Blanc to end their interest in the competition at that stage.

Paraguay showed that France '98 was no fluke by qualifying comfortably this time round. They finished second to Argentina in the South America

The Finals
Group B
v South Africa
v Spain
v Slovenia

group, drawing both games against one of the tournament's hot favourites. Argentina coach Marcelo Bielsa paid tribute to the Paraguayans after the two matches, commenting that they were his side's toughest opponents in the 10-nation group.

This summer, Paraguay will once again face Spain in the opening phase. Having gone through at Spain's expense four years ago, Paraguay won't fear them this time. Even if they lose out to Jose Camacho's team, Paraguay should advance to the second round. They are ranked much higher than Slovenia and South Africa, the other countries in Group B.

One drawback will be that they will have to line up against South Africa and Spain without Chilavert. He will be serving a suspension, following a fracas with Brazil's Roberto Carlos during a volatile qualifier last August. That means Paraguay will lose their portly talisman, and the man who notched four goals for them on the road to the World Cup.

Path to the Finals

Peru 2 Paraguay 0
Paraguay 1 Uruguay 0
Paraguay 3 Ecuador 1
Chile 3 Paraguay 1
Paraguay 2 Brazil 1
Bolivia 0 Paraguay 0
Argentina 1 Paraguay 1
Paraguay 3 Venezuela 0
Colombia 0 Paraguay 2
Paraguay 5 Peru 1
Uruguay 0 Paraguay 1
Ecuador 2 Paraguay 1
Paraguay 1 Chile 0
Brazil 2 Paraguay 0
Paraguay 5 Bolivia 1
Paraguay 2 Argentina 2
Venezuela 3 Paraguay 1
Paraguay 0 Colombia 4

Paraguay's Carlos Espinola challenges Ivan Kaviedes of Ecuador.

Poland

Since the heady days of 1970s and early 1980s, when Poland twice reached the semi-finals of the World Cup, it has been in the footballing doldrums. The country which broke the hearts of England fans in 1973 has failed to reach the last three World Cups.

Poland's fortunes have been revitalised in recent years, and they are now showing the kind of form that made them such a threat two decades ago.

A potentially tricky qualifying group pitted Poland against Ukraine, Belarus, Norway, Wales and Armenia. Ukraine had the superb Shevchenko-Rebrov strike partnership, while Norway who made it to the knockout stage at France '98 boasted several Premiership stars. Poland came through relatively comfortably. Their campaign included excellent away wins against Ukraine and Norway. The only reverse came in Belarus, where they went down 4-1.

The Finals
Group D
v South Korea
v Portugal
v USA

The man everyone is talking about in the Polish side is Emmanuel Olisadebe. Twenty-three-year-old Olisadebe was born in Nigeria but is an adopted son of Poland, having gained citizenship of the country two years ago. His application was said to have been given fast-track treatment, on the orders of the President. Poland was taking no chances, and they wanted his status confirmed so that he would be eligible for the World Cup qualifying campaign.

Olisadebe made the decision to play for Poland because he felt he was being overlooked by the country of his birth. With seven goals in the qualifiers, he quickly began repaying the Polish football authorities for the faith that they showed in him. Nigeria's loss was undoubtedly Poland's gain.

Even without their star acquisition, Poland would probably fancy themselves to progress to the second round with Portugal, at the expense of the USA and South Korea. If Olisadebe maintains his hot scoring form, and Liverpool keeper Jerzy Dudek can keep the door shut at the back, Poland should reach the knockout stage for the first time since 1986.

Pavel Kryszatowicz of Poland takes the ball past Kit Symons during the Group Five Qualifying game against Wales. Poland won the match 2-1.

Path to the Finals

Ukraine 1 Poland 3
Poland 3 Belarus 1
Poland 0 Wales 0
Norway 2 Poland 3
Poland 4 Armenia 0
Wales 1 Poland 2
Armenia 1 Poland 1
Poland 3 Norway 0
Belarus 4 Poland 1
Poland 1 Ukraine 1

Portugal

The clock is running for the wonderfully talented Portuguese side. Many of the present squad came through the ranks of the youth team which won FIFA's Under-20 World Championship in 1989 and 1991. By 1996, when England hosted the European Championship, stars such as Luis Figo and Manuel Rui Costa were established in the senior side. Portugal were hugely entertaining, but went out to Czechoslovakia at the semi-final stage. Another chance of glory fell by the wayside two years later, when Portugal didn't even make it to the World Cup in France. It was the last four again in Euro 2000. Nuno Gomes put Portugal ahead in the match, against world champions France. But Thierry Henry equalised, and Zinedine Zidane scored an extra-time Golden Goal from the penalty spot to put France into the final.

With several of their top players now at their peak, this World Cup represents Portugal's best hope of winning a major tournament.

The first task was to ensure that the mistakes of the last World Cup weren't repeated. That was accomplished as they finished top of their qualifying

The Finals
Group D
v USA
v Poland
v South Korea

group, unbeaten. Mick McCarthy's Republic of Ireland side did well to match Portugal's record of seven wins and three draws, and put Holland out of the competition in the process. The big difference between the two qualifiers was in the striking department: Portugal blasted 33 goals in the 10-match series, 10 more than the Republic. It isn't for nothing but they have been dubbed the Brazil of European football.

Portugal have the quality to go all the way in the tournament. They will go into the competition with World Player of the Year in Luis Figo. Can he and the other gifted individuals help Portugal finally shake off the "attractive losers" tag this time round?

Path to the Finals

Estonia 1 Portugal 3
Portugal 1 Ireland 1
Holland 0 Portugal 2
Portugal 3 Andorra 0
Portugal 2 Holland 2
Ireland 1 Portugal 1
Portugal 6 Cyprus 0
Andorra 1 Portugal 7
Cyprus 1 Portugal 3
Portugal 5 Estonia 0

Joao Pinto receives the congratulations as he scores during the Group Two Qualifying game against Cyprus. Portugal won the match 6-0.

Russia

The Finals

Group H
v Belgium
v Japan
v Tunisia

Russia lost just once on their way to topping a qualifying group that included Slovenia, Switzerland and Yugoslavia. Their only reverse came in Slovenia, where the Russians went down 2-1. They confirmed their place in Japan and Korea and consigned Slovenia to the play-offs with an emphatic 4-0 home win over Switzerland in early October. Two of their key players grabbed the goals. Vladimir Beschastnykh hit a first-half hat-trick, with playmaker Igor Titov putting the icing on the cake with a fourth late in the game.

Russia has only featured as an independent footballing nation for the past ten years, following the break-up of the Soviet Union. There were disappointing early exits in the first major tournaments of the new era, USA '94 and Euro '96. Russia didn't feature at all in the finals of France '98 and Euro 2000.

Russia's coach, Oleg Romantsev, is playing down his side's World Cup chances, saying that they lack the quality and physical attributes to do well in the tournament. East European teams are notoriously poor travellers, which won't help Romantsev's cause. Russia does have some classy players, though. As well as Beschastnykh and Titov, there is Marat Izmailov, Lokomotiv Moscow's teenage midfield player who is reportedly on the shopping list of some of the big-name clubs from western Europe. The national team goalkeeper is Ruslan Nigmatullin, who also plays for Lokomotiv. He has been in excellent form; in 2000 he set a record for his country by going 939 minutes without conceding a goal.

Despite some quality individual performers, Russia is unlikely to have a big impact on the tournament. The country was favoured by the draw, however. With Japan as the seeded side in Group H, the Russians may fancy their chances of taking one of the top two slots, alongside Belgium or Tunisia.

Vladimir Beschastnykh of Russia in action against Luxemburg

Path to the Finals

Switzerland 0 Russia 1
Russia 3 Luxembourg 0
Russia 1 Slovenia 1
Russia 1 Faroe Islands 0
Yugoslavia 0 Russia 1
Russia 1 Yugoslavia 1
Luxembourg 1 Russia 2
Slovenia 2 Russia 1
Faroe Islands 0 Russia 3
Russia 4 Switzerland 0

Saudia Arabia

The standard of Asian football, like that of Africa, is improving all the time. Saudi Arabia is the strongest footballing nation in this increasingly competitive region. Its team has reached the last five Asian cup finals, a record stretching back 18 years. Saudi Arabia won the tournament in 1984, 1988 and 1996, and finished runner-up in 1992 and 2000.

The Saudi team has also made its mark at World Cup level. At USA '94 the team made it to the second round, after recording wins over Morocco and Belgium, and only going down 2-1 to Holland. Sweden halted their progress at the knockout stage, the Saudis losing 3-1. Even so, Saudi Arabia had the distinction of becoming the first Asian team to make it through the group stage since North Korea's famous exploits of 1966.

France '98 wasn't such a happy experience. The Saudis finished bottom of a group including the host nation the eventual winners and Denmark, who reached the last eight. South Africa was the other country in Saudi Arabia's group, and that game ended in a 2-2 draw, giving the Saudis their only point of the tournament. Saudi Arabia reached this year's finals by topping a group comprising

The Finals
Group E
v Germany
v Cameroon
v Ireland

Iran, Iraq, Bahrain and Thailand. Iran ran them the closest. The Iranians were in the driving seat going into the last round of matches. A win in Bahrain would have taken them to the finals, irrespective of what Saudi Arabia did in their home game against Thailand. The Saudis duly won their match 4-1. They needed Bahrain to do them a favour, and their Arab neighbours obliged, beating Iran 3-1.

Iran was left to face the Republic of Ireland in a play-off, which Mick McCarthy's side won. The Saudis will come up against the Republic in Group E, with Germany and Cameroon providing the other opposition. The Saudis are the outsiders of the group, and the fortune they enjoyed in qualifying won't do anything to shorten their odds. On the positive side, the team will know it can win at World Cup level. And realistically, there won't to be too great a burden of expectation on the players' shoulders. But the fervent Saudi fans have already had a taste of second-round glory, and will want their team to repeat that achievement.

Path to the Finals

Saudi Arabia 6 Mongolia 0
Bangladesh 0 Saudi Arabia 3
Saudi Arabia 5 Vietnam 0
Saudi Arabia 6 Mongolia 0
Saudi Arabia 6 Bangladesh 0
Saudi Arabia 4 Vietnam 0
Saudi Arabia 1 Bahrain 1
Iran 2 Saudi Arabia 0
Saudi Arabia 1 Iraq 0
Thailand 1 Saudi Arabia 3
Bahrain 0 Saudi Arabia 4
Saudi Arabia 2 Iran 2
Saudi Arabia 4 Thailand 0

Saudi Arabia's Sami Al takes on Jassem Yousef of Qatar in the qualifier in Doha, Qatar.

Senegal

Senegal will go into the World Cup as the rank outsiders. Along with China, Slovenia, and Ecuador, Senegal will be making their first appearance in the finals. On paper - and in FIFA's rankings Senegal is the weakest of the 32 teams. They have profited from the fact that FIFA now awards five places to African sides. On a brighter note, Senegal topped what was probably the continent's toughest qualifying group. It included Morocco, Egypt and Algeria - all of whom have made it to the finals before.

Senegal will feature in the tournament's curtain-raiser. The eyes of the world will be on them as they take on reigning champions France. It will be a daunting task, and a game which will have a twist of irony. For while the top stars of the French side are playing in Italy, Spain and England, the majority of Senegal's players are with French clubs.

Two of Senegal's best performers are strikers El Hadji

The Finals
Group A
v France
v Denmark
v Uruguay

Diouf and Khalilou Fadida, who play for Lens and Auxerre respectively. Another is coach Bruno Metsu, who is also a Frenchman. He acquired hero status as he masterminded the team's excellent run in the qualifying series. There were wild celebrations when Senegal booked its place for Japan and Korea. Even the country's president joined in, cutting short a state visit. Metsu insists that Senegal aren't just going to the World Cup to make up the numbers. He thinks his side will be as colourful and entertaining as Jamaica's "Reggae Boys" were at France 98 but with a steelier resolve. Jamaica went down to Croatia and Argentina, then beat Japan to finish third four years ago. Senegal might find it difficult to match that achievement. Uruguay and Denmark, their other group opponents, are countries with impressive international pedigrees. Ever the optimist, Metsu still believes that qualification to the second round is a realistic possibility.

Senegal's chances would have been better had Metsu been able to field Patrick Vieira, who was born in the country. That confrontation will be an interesting subplot to the main theme: getting three points in your opening game. On that score, Senegal is unlikely to repeat Cameroon's fantastic achievement in 1990, when they beat champions Argentina in the opening match.

Ousseinoh Diouf of Senegal during the game against Egypt played in Cairo.

Path to the Finals

Algeria 1 Senegal 1
Senegal 0 Egypt 0
Morocco 0 Senegal 0
Senegal 4 Namibia 0
Senegal 3 Algeria 0
Egypt 1 Senegal 0
Senegal 1 Morocco 0
Namibia 0 Senegal 5

Slovenia

Many casual observers will be quick to consign Slovenia to the role of also-rans. That could be a mistake, as this young country has an impressive track record over the past couple of years.

Slovenia emerged from the break-up of Yugoslavia in 1991, and was admitted to FIFA the following year. The country's progress on the football field has been steady, if unspectacular. Euro '96 was Slovenia's competitive debut, and they finished fifth out of six in their qualifying group. They failed to make it to France '98, too, but since then there have been some hugely encouraging performances.

Slovenia made it to their first major tournament when they qualified for Euro 2000. Although they finished bottom of their group, that doesn't tell the full story. The opening fixture pitted them against Yugoslavia, and gave the game an added edge. After an hour, Slovenia were 3-0 up, only to concede three late goals and have to settle for a point. In their second match, they lost narrowly to the big guns of Spain,

The Finals

Group B
v Spain
v South Africa
v Paraguay

and then played out a goalless draw with Norway.

Slovenia have not lost since that defeat against Spain whom they will meet again in this summer's World Cup. They came through a very tight qualifying group. Five wins and five draws from their ten games put them second to Russia in the final table. Russia lost once to the Slovenes but seven wins put them in the driving seat. Yugoslavia, meanwhile, came close to matching Slovenia's record, with five wins and four draws. A home defeat by Russia was the critical difference, and Slovenia finished one point ahead. Second place meant a play-off against Romania. Romania beat England at France '98 and Euro 2000, and went into the game as favourites, yet it was Slovenia who came through.

Even if the form book prevails and Slovenia lose again to Spain again this summer, they could still make it to the knockout stage. The Slovenes ought to be too strong for South Africa, and could well edge out the higher-ranked Paraguay for the second qualifying spot in Group B.

Path to the Finals

Faroe Islands 2 Slovenia 2
Luxembourg 1 Slovenia 2
Slovenia 2 Switzerland 2
Russia 1 Slovenia 1
Slovenia 1 Yugoslavia 1
Slovenia 2 Luxembourg 0
Switzerland 0 Slovenia 1
Slovenia 2 Russia 1
Yugoslavia 1 Slovenia 1
Slovenia 3 Faroe Islands 0

Play off
1st Leg
Slovenia 2 Romania 1
2nd Leg
Romania 1 Slovenia 1

Slovenia
win on aggregate 3 - 2

Slovenia's Zeljko Milinovic clears the ball as Ioan Ganea of Romania closes in.

South Africa

South outh Africa has wasted little time since returning to the international footballing fold in 1992. That was the year that FIFA re-admitted the country to its ranks, after 28 years in the sporting wilderness during the apartheid era.

Bafana Bafana, as the national side is known, won the prestigious African Nations Cup in 1996, then qualified for the World Cup two years later. Elimination came at the first hurdle, but the team left France with some credit. They recovered from a 3-0 defeat by the powerhouse host country to gain noteworthy draws against Denmark and Saudi Arabia.

The Finals

Group B
v Paraguay
v Slovenia
v Spain

South Africa's coach is Carlos Queiroz, the man who guided Portugal to the World Youth championship in 1991. He may not have the quality of a Figo or Rui Costa at his disposal now, but he will certainly get the best from the talent available to him.

One significant blow for Queiroz could be that his former captain Lucas Radebe might not recover from injury in time for the tournament. Radebe and Queiroz had already fallen out over club vs country commitments, a rift which resulted in the coach handing the captaincy of Bafana Bafana to Charlton's Shaun Bartlett. He wouldn't have wanted to lose Radebe as a player, though. The Leeds defender has been dogged by injury for much of the past year, and his presence in Japan and Korea must now be in severe doubt.

Assuming that Spain don't implode yet again in a major tournament, South Africa will be vying for the second qualifying spot along with Slovenia and Paraguay. Both the FIFA rankings and the bookmakers have them finishing bottom of the group. The World Cup has a habit of throwing up teams that upset the form books however; Queiroz will be out to make South Africa one of the surprise packages of the tournament.

Quinton Fortune (left) of South Africa brushes aside Vicenzo Montella during match against Italy in Perugia.

Path to the Finals

Zimbabwe 0 South Africa 2
South Africa 1 Burkina Faso 0
Malawi 1 South Africa 2
South Africa 2 Zimbabwe 1
Burkina Faso 1 South Africa 1
South Africa 2 Malawi 0

South Korea

2002 will be South Korea's fifth consecutive appearance at the World Cup. Despite being one of the strongest footballing nations in Asia, South Korea has yet to register a victory on the biggest stage. In the 12 matches they played in the last four tournaments, the Koreans drew four and lost the rest. The country's best performance came at USA '94, where the team took a point off Spain and Bolivia, and only went down 3-2 to Germany. Two points obviously wasn't enough to secure qualification, but at least it lifted the country into third place in the group, the only time that South Korea has avoided finishing bottom.

Star players are somewhat thin on the ground for this summer's co-hosts. Much will depend on the form of Lee Dong Gook, the country's premier striker, who top scored with six goals in the 2000 Asian Cup. Seol Ki-Hyeon is another player expected to do well. He has benefited from playing in Belgium for several seasons, and joined champions Anderlecht last summer.

Perhaps the country's most important figure, however, is their coach, Guus Hiddink. The appointment of the former PSV Eindhoven coach, in January 2001, marked a significant departure for South Korea. Until then, the country had employed only home-based coaches; Hiddink's arrival marked a recognition by South Korea's footballing authorities that an experienced European coach would help their development.

Success is always relative. South Korea's initial aim will be to record their first World Cup victory. That looks unlikely to come against either Portugal or Poland, and the USA are also much higher in the FIFA rankings. It is hard to see South Korea improving significantly on their past record. It will be a huge shock if the co-hosts don't bow out of the competition at the first hurdle.

The Finals
Group D
v Poland
v USA
v Portugal

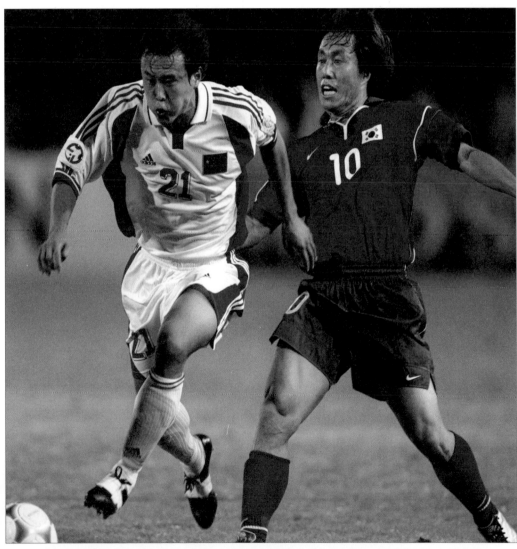

Xu Yunglong of China goes past Noh Jung-Yoon of South Korea during the Asian Cup Third Place playoff match.

Spain

Spain are the perennial under achievers of world football. Fourth place in the 1950 World Cup is the best the country has managed in nine appearances in the finals. The latter, along with a European championship win on home soil in 1964, represents a poor return for a football-mad country which has never been short of talent.

If this has been a general pattern of the post-war era, then it is particularly true now. Deportivo La Coruna, Celta Vigo, Alaves, Real Mallorca and Valencia have all proved themselves to be formidable opposition in Europe over the past few years. The depth of the Primera Liga now goes much further than Barcelona and the two Madrid sides. It is widely accepted

The Finals

Group B
v Slovenia
v Paraguay
v South Africa

that Spain currently has the strongest domestic league in Europe, and that country's fans will undoubtedly feel that it is about time the success of the clubs was replicated at international level.

At Euro '96 Spain came up against England and David Seaman on one of their better days as far as penalty shoot-outs were concerned. If that was disappointing, then it paled in comparison to France '98, where defeat by Nigeria and a draw against Paraguay sent them crashing out at the group stage. At Euro 2000 the team made it to the last eight, where they went down 2-1 to eventual winners France. Star striker Raul, of all people, missed a last-minute penalty to pile on the agony.

Qualification for Japan and Korea was achieved at a canter, although a group including Austria, Israel, Bosnia-Herzegovina and Liechtenstein hardly provided the sternest test.

Spain will renew their acquaintance with Paraguay this summer. Slovenia and South Africa complete the group, and it is hard to see Spain slipping up at the first hurdle again. Once they reach the knockout stages, Spain will provide dangerous opposition for anyone.

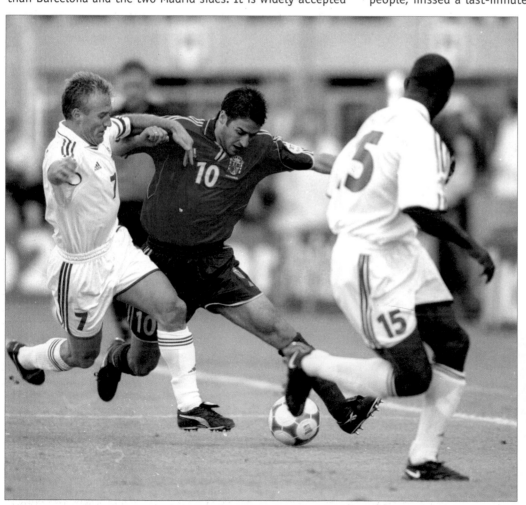

Raul beats Didier Deschamps of France during the European Championships 2000 Quarter Finals match.

Path to the Finals

Bosnia-Herzegovina 1 Spain 2
Spain 2 Israel 0
Austria 1 Spain 1
Spain 5 Liechtenstein 0
Spain 4 Bosnia-Herzegovina 1
Israel 1 Spain 1
Spain 4 Austria 0
Liechtenstein 2 Spain 0

Sweden

Sweden has a chequered World Cup history. They have reached the finals once, in 1958 on home territory. Unfortunately, they came up against an awesome Brazil side, inspired by 17-year-old Pele, and lost 5-2.

In the next 32 years, Sweden made it to the World Cup just four times, and only got past the opening stage once.

At Italia '90 the side lost to Brazil, Scotland and Costa Rica to continue a miserable run. Things then took a turn for the better. Sweden reached the semi-finals of the 1992 European championship, knocking out England along the way. They then got to the last four in the World Cup two years later. As in 1958, they lost to Brazil, but this time by a single goal.

The rollercoaster took another dip after these two fine achievements. Sweden failed to reach France '98, and finished bottom of their group at Euro 2000.

Unfortunately for England, the graph has taken another upward turn in the last couple of years. They qualified for Japan and Korea without losing a single game. The six-team group contained three weak countries, but Turkey and Slovakia were in there to provide stiffer opposition.

The Finals

Group F
v England
v Nigeria
v Argentina

Despite such a patchy overall record, England fans won't need to be reminded that their team has failed to beat Sweden in eight attempts, stretching back to 1968. The most recent clash ended 1-1 last November, with Sweden missing three of their top players. Henrik Larsson last year's Golden Boot winner and Freddie Ljungberg are well known to England supporters. The other player unavailable on that occasion was influential captain Patrick Andersson. This classy defender won the Champions League with Bayern Munich last year before moving to Barcelona in the summer.

Sweden's strength lies more in excellent teamwork thanindividual stars. However. Sven-Goran Eriksson will know better than anyone how resilient and hard to beat his native country is.

Path to the Finals

Azerbaijan 0 Sweden 1
Sweden 1 Turkey 1
Slovakia 0 Sweden 0
Sweden 1 Macedonia 0
Moldova 0 Sweden 2
Sweden 2 Slovakia 0
Sweden 6 Moldova 0
Macedonia 1 Sweden 2
Turkey 1 Sweden 2
Sweden 3 Azerbaijan 0

Sweden celebrate scoring a goal during the Qualifier against Slovakia in Stockholm.

Tunisia

This summer will mark Tunisia's third World Cup appearance. The country's debut was in Argentina in 1978, and the team acquitted itself extremely well. The 3-1 win over Mexico marked the first ever victory for an African team at the finals. They followed it up with a fine 0-0 draw against Germany, who only finished a point ahead of Tunisia in second place in the group.

It was another 20 years before Tunisia reached the finals again. They lost to England in their opening game at France '98, and were also beaten by Colombia, before notching a point from their last group match against Romania. Although Tunisia finished bottom of the group, they had again done

The Finals

Group H
v Russia
v Belgium
v Japan

reasonably well against some quality opposition.

Many of the players from France '98 will be there again this summer, making an experienced unit which won't be a pushover for anybody. The team's goalkeeper and captain, Chokri El Ouaer, is one of Tunisia's veterans and remains a key figure. There is new blood, too, with the likes of Hassen Gabsi, Ali Zitouni and Ziad Jaziri, who are some of the rising stars of African football.

Tunisia topped a group including the Ivory Coast, DR Congo, Madagascar and Congo to book their place for Japan and Korea. Nigeria and Cameroon will be regarded as having the best chance of the five-strong African contingent, but Tunisia will be tricky opponents for Japan, Belgium and Russia. The lack of a big-name seed makes this one of the closest groups. Just 15 places separates all four teams in the FIFA rankings. Belgium, at 20, are the highest-ranked country, with Russia at 22 and Japan at 35. Tunisia, who are currently ranked 28, must feel they have an excellent chance of making it third time lucky and progressing to the second round.

Tunisia's Adel Selimi in action during the CAF 2nd Round Qualifier between Tunisia and the Ivory Coast.

Path to the Finals

Ivory Coast 2 Tunisia 2
Tunisia 1 Madagascar 0
Congo 1 Tunisia 2
Tunisia 6 Congo DR 0
Madagascar 0 Tunisia 2
Tunisia 1 Ivory Coast 1
Tunisia 6 Congo 0
Congo DR 0 Tunisia 3

Turkey

Turkey is a country whose World Cup pedigree does not give a true reflection of its teams current potential. Turkey has only one previous appearance in the finals to its credit, and that was way back in 1954. But over the past decade, Turkish football has made significant strides, both at club and international level. Turkey broke a 42-year run of failing to reach the finals of a major tournament when the team made it to Euro '96. The Turks made a swift exit, with neither a point nor a goal to their name, but it was a sign of better things to come. At Euro 2000, Turkey finished above Belgium and Sweden to qualify for the second round, where the country was knocked out by Portugal.

This progress has been matched at club level. Galatasaray has regularly featured in the Champions League, and no visiting team relishes the prospect of a trip to Istanbul. The country's premier club side has also had some impressive results on its travels. Galatasaray memorably scored three times at Old Trafford during the 1994 European Cup campaign, enough to dump Alex Ferguson's men out on the away goals rule.

The greatest fillip for Turkish football came two years ago. Eliminated from the Champions League, Galatasaray entered the UEFA Cup and went on to lift the trophy, beating Arsenal in the final.

To qualify for this summer's World Cup, Turkey finished second to Sweden in their group, then beat Austria in a play-off. Coach Senol Gunes draws many of his players from Galatasaray and the other two big clubs in the domestic league, Besiktas and Fenerbahce. There are also some quality performers who have made their mark in other European leagues, notably Alpay at Aston Villa, Tugay at Blackburn and Leicester's Muzzy Izzet. Turkey's biggest star is striker Hakan Sukur, whose performances for Galatasaray and the national team prompted Inter Milan to take him to Italy two years ago.

Turkey is ranked higher than China and Costa Rica in Group C, and the country should repeat its Euro 2000 achievement of progressing to the knockout stage this summer.

The Finals

Group C
v Brazil
v Costa Rica
v China

Path to the Finals

Turkey 2 Moldova 0
Sweden 1 Turkey 1
Azerbaijan 0 Turkey 1
Turkey 1 Slovakia 2
Macedonia 1 Turkey 2
Turkey 3 Azerbaijan 0
Turkey 3 Macedonia 3
Slovakia 0 Turkey 1
Turkey 1 Sweden 2
Moldova 0 Turkey 3

Play off
1st Leg
Austria 0 Turkey 1
2nd Leg
Turkey 5 Austria 0

Turkey win
on aggregate 6 - 0

Hasan Sas of Turkey is tackled by Tobias Linderoth during the World Cup Qualifier between Turkey and Sweden played at the Ali Sami Yen Stadium in Istanbul.

USA

The USA will make it four World Cups in a row when the team lines up against Portugal, Poland and South Korea this summer. In two of the country's three previous appearances, Italia '90 and France '98, the USA failed to register a single point. 1994 was the high point of the modern era. With home advantage, the team drew with Switzerland and beat Colombia to make it through to the second phase. They went out to eventual winners Brazil at that stage, though only by a single goal.

The USA's World Cup adventure didn't begin in 1990, however. A team from the States featured in three of the first four tournaments. They made it to the semi-finals of the inaugural competition in 1930, although it has to be remembered that only 13 teams participated in that year. In 1934, when the tournament was run on a straight knockout basis throughout, the USA were thrashed 7-1 by Italy in their one and only match. In 1950, the USA again went out at the first hurdle, but they did record that historic 1-0 win over a powerful England side. There was then a 40-year hiatus before Italia '90 ushered

The Finals
Group D
v Portugal
v South Korea
v Poland

in a new era for American football.

Qualification this time round was not overly impressive. A scratchy 2-1 win over Jamaica sealed the country's place in their penultimate group match, but they were helped by other results going their way. The USA had expected to have to go to Trinidad and get a result in their final match; now that wasn't necessary. When the last round of matches was completed, the USA took the third qualifying spot, behind Costa Rica and Mexico.

The USA's biggest name player is their captain Claudio Reyna, who moved from Rangers to Sunderland just before Christmas. Other players England fans will be familiar with are Everton's Joe-Max Moore and Blackburn 'keeper Brad Friedel. Another man to watch is teenage sensation Landon Donovan.

Coach Bruce Arena is playing down the USA's chances in Japan and Korea. He feels that a big breakthrough is still many years away. For now, success will be matching the achievement of 1994 and getting through the first round. That won't be easy. On paper, the USA should beat South Korea, and they are even ranked above Poland. That is a quirk of FIFA's ranking system, however, and the bookmakers are offering long odds on the USA getting through at the expense of either Poland or Portugal, Group D's seeded team.

Goalkeeper Oscar Perez of Mexico gets to the ball ahead of Ernie Stewart of USA during 2nd Round Qualifier played at the Azteca Stadium in Mexico City

Path to the Finals
USA 2 Mexico 0
Honduras 1 USA 2
USA 1 Costa Rica 0
Jamaica 0 USA 0
USA 2 Trinidad & Tobago 0
Mexico 1 USA 0
USA 2 Honduras 3
Costa Rica 2 USA 0
USA 2 Jamaica 1
Trinidad & Tobago 0 USA 0

Uruguay

Uruguay's proud World Cup record is somewhat unbalanced. The South Americans enjoyed two victories in the first four tournaments, and were one of the strongest footballing nations of the pre-war era.

Since that last victory, in 1950, things haven't gone so well. Of the 12 tournaments that took place between 1954 and 1998, Brazil and Argentina won six between them. Over the same period, Uruguay were left in the shadows. Two 4th-place finishes in 1954 and 1970 were Uruguay's best performances over this 44-year stretch. On five occasions they didn't even make it to the finals.

Uruguay's appearance this summer will be their first since Italia '90. And that was in the balance as they only scraped into fifth place in South America's 10-nation group. With the first four countries gaining automatic qualification, Uruguay had to come through a tense play-off against Australia to book their place in the finals.

When they put out Kewell, Viduka and co. to complete the 32-team line-up for Japan and Korea, Uruguay ensured that all seven countries who have won the competition in its 72-year history will be present this summer.

Few will give Uruguay much chance against reigning champions France, whom they meet at the group stage. But with Denmark and Senegal providing the other opposition, the South Americans must fancy their chances of reaching the knockout stage for the first time since 1970.

Several of Uruguay's top players are with European club sides. Fabian Carini, their highly-rated 'keeper is at Juventus, and top striker Dario Silva plays for Malaga. England fans may see one familiar face in the Uruguay ranks as Tottenham's Gustavo Poyet looks likely to make the squad.

The Finals

Group A

v Denmark
v France
v Senegal

Path to the Finals

Uruguay 1 Bolivia 0
Paraguay 1 Uruguay 0
Uruguay 2 Chile 1
Brazil 1 Uruguay 1
Uruguay 3 Venezuela 1
Uruguay 0 Peru 0
Colombia 1 Uruguay 0
Uruguay 4 Ecuador 0
Argentina 2 Uruguay 1
Bolivia 0 Uruguay 0
Uruguay 0 Paraguay 1
Chile 0 Uruguay 1
Uruguay 1 Brazil 0
Venezuela 2 Uruguay 2
Peru 0 Uruguay 0
Uruguay 1 Colombia 1
Ecuador 1 Uruguay 1
Uruguay 1 Argentina 1

Play-off
1st Leg
Australia 1 Uruguay 0
2nd Leg
Uruguay 3 Australia 0

Uruguay win
on aggregate 3-1

Mark Viduka of Australia is outnumbered by the Uruguay defence during the play-off second leg match played in Montevideo. Uruguay won 3-0, and qualified for the World Cup Finals with a 3-1 aggregate win.

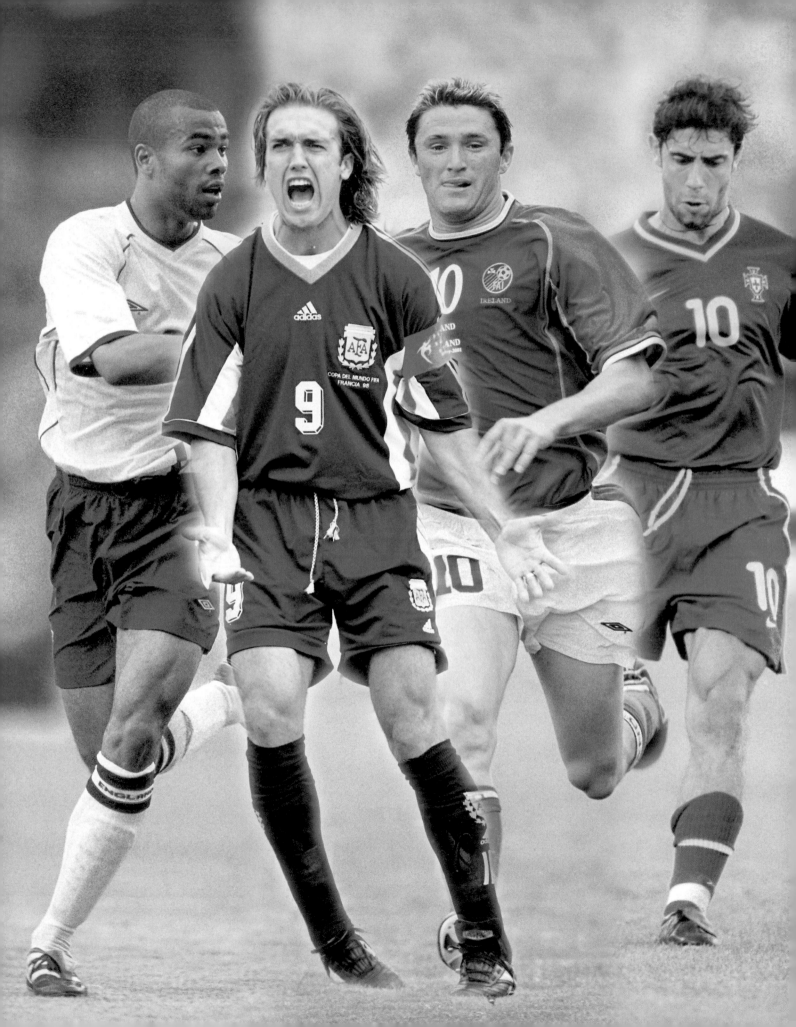

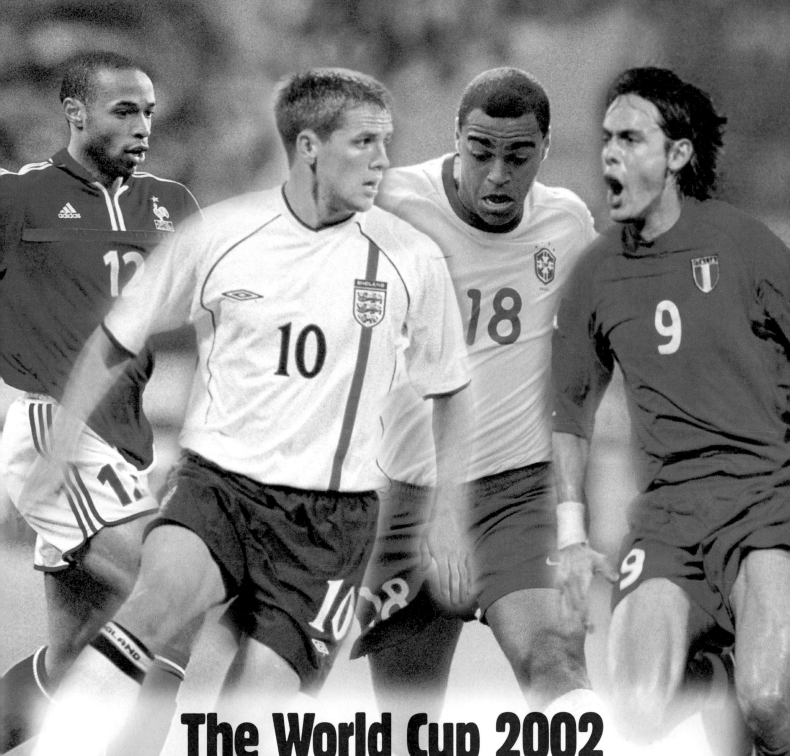

The World Cup 2002
The Players

Germany's hot-shot

Germany

Michael Ballack has already done enough to earn the undying gratitude of Germany's fans. He played a huge part in helping to protect his country's proud record of appearing in every World Cup since 1954. Ballack's away goal in the play-off against the Ukraine earned Germany a 1-1 draw, and set up the storming victory in the home leg a few days later. Ballack hit two more in that game, which finished 4-1, and Germany were able to make their travel plans for Japan and Korea.

Even before those three vital strikes, Ballack was being feted as the hottest property in German football. Terrific technically, and a wonderful passer of the ball, 25-year-old Ballack is also the man Bayer Leverkusen look to for leadership. Few doubt that he will now go on to become the focal point of the national team, and this year's World Cup will be the first big opportunity for him to show whether he is ready to take on that responsibility.

Born in East Germany, Ballack spent his early years in the GDR's youth system. He signed for Chemnitz when he was 14, the same year that the two Germanys reunited. It meant that West Germany already the most successful international side in post-war history now had the best of East German talent to draw on too.

Ballack was spotted by scouts for Bundesliga side Kaiserslautern, and that looked like the next step up in his meteoric rise. There was a blip, though, for he fell out with coach Otto Rehhagel. In 1999, he found himself frozen out, spending a lot of his time on the bench. He had already broken into the national side; and being left out at club level obviously threatened his international career.

The deadlock was broken when he was within months of completing his contract and becoming a free agent under the Bosman rule. Kaiserslautern opted to let him go early and get a fee. Bayer Leverkusen could have strung out negotiations to get Ballack for nothing, but they were so keen to make sure they got their man that they handed over £3 million.

Now it is Leverkusen who are struggling to keep him. Bayern Munich are reported to be favourites to sign him, beating off the interest of many of Europe's top sides. He is under long-term contract at Leverkusen, but there is a clause allowing him to move in 2002 if a club is prepared to stump up £8 million. If he does go to Bayern, he could become the successor to the majestic Steffan Effenberg. Effenberg agrees he is the man to take over as the leader of Bayern's pack. Should he also become the lynch-pin of the German side, he will go one better than Effenberg, whose own international career has been blighted by a long-standing dispute.

Michael Ballack

England

England's favourite on the left

The left side of midfield has proved to be the thorniest problem for England's managers in recent years. Many players have been tried there, but Nick Barmby looks favourite to start in that position when the serious business gets under way in Japan and Korea - providing he can regain his fitness. Last October, it was confirmed that he needed an ankle operation which would keep him out until the new year. It must have been a huge blow to Barmby, who had been in such good form since joining Liverpool in the summer of 2000.

With his £6 million move to Anfield, Barmby finally achieved what he had first attempted ten years earlier. He had a two-week trial at Liverpool as a teenager, but failed to make an impression. Spurs took him on instead, and it was at White Hart Lane that he made his mark as one of the brightest young talents in the land. At 18, he broke into Ossie Ardiles's flamboyant, attacking Spurs team, playing alongside Teddy Sheringham, Darren Anderton and Jurgen Klinsmann.

Spurs fans were stunned in 1995, when the Hull-born player decided he wanted to return to his northern roots. Bryan Robson took him to Middlesbrough, but Barmby spent just a single, turbulent season at the Riverside before he was on the move again. Liverpool was the next port of call but it was the blue half of the city which celebrated Joe Royle's big-money acquisition. Four more rollercoaster years at Goodison followed. His form waxed and waned, as did the fortunes of the club. During the 1999-2000 season, he strung together a run of scintillating performances which earned him a recall to the England squad, after four years in the international wilderness. A couple of appearances followed in the ill-fated Euro 2000 campaign. It was immediately after that tournament that he left Goodison for Anfield, becoming the first Everton player for over 40 years to swap the blue shirt for the red of their arch-rivals.

Did You Know

Nick Barmby became the first player to move from Everton to Liverpool since striker Dave Hickson made the short trip across Stanley Park back in 1959.

Nick Barmby

The eccentric genius

France

Think of Fabien Barthez and two things immediately spring to mind. The ritual kiss planted on his bald head by team-mate Laurent Blanc before international matches; and the succession of howlers that have led to his fall from grace this season.

Barthez joined Manchester United in the summer of 2000 with a formidable pedigree: he had just won the French championship with Monaco for the second time; he had a European Cup winners medal to his name, won with his previous club, Marseille, in 1993; he was a key member of the team which triumphed at France '98, then went on to be crowned kings of Europe two years later; and he was the undisputed number one 'keeper in world football.

Barthez's first season at Old Trafford merely enhanced his reputation. He was in scintillating form as he marshalled the meanest defence in the Premiership to yet another league title. This season it's all gone horribly wrong. There has still been a healthy quota of stupendous saves, but these have been punctuated by too many howlers. United's visit to Highbury at the end of November was typical: a string of great saves, then two terrible blunders late in the game which presented Thierry Henry with an open net. United went down to their fourth defeat of the season, 3-1. Gooners fans loved it, of course, while there were also rumblings of discontent among the Old Trafford faithful.

Manchester United and Alex Ferguson are renowned for never resting on their laurels. Time and again, the Old Trafford machine has shown its readiness to dispense with the services of any player who falls short of the very highest standards. Thirty-year-old Barthez's position now looks under severe threat. As far as the World Cup is concerned, which 'keeper will be on show: the eccentric genius or the eccentric liability?

Fabien Barthez

Argentina's all-time best

Argentina

The nickname says it all: Batigol. It was bestowed on Gabriel Batistuta by his adoring fans at Fiorentina, the club where he performed so brilliantly for ten seasons. In that time, he proved himself to be the scourge of Serie A defences. But it was for his loyalty, as well as his goalscoring feats, that Batistuta was revered at Fiorentina. He stuck with the club when they were relegated in 1993. He helped them win promotion back into the top flight at the first attempt, and soon afterwards, a statue was erected in his name.

Unfortunately for such a great player, that was one of the few honours he achieved at Fiorentina. Victories in the Coppa Italia and Italian Super Cup were scant reward for his immense contribution over so many years.

Batistuta finally made the decision to move on in 2000, when he joined Roma in a £23 million deal. The prized Scudetto came in his first year at his new club, with Batistuta credited for bringing a decisive extra touch of class up front.

His record at international level is no less impressive. He became Argentina's all-time record goalscorer in the qualifying series leading up to France '98. Then, at the tournament itself, he hit an 11-minute hat-trick, Jamaica the unfortunate side on the receiving end. He ended the competition with five goals, making him joint-second top scorer behind Davor Suker.

More recently, he has had his differences with the national team management. Last autumn, when Argentina played Paraguay in a qualifier for this year's competition, Batistuta was included for the first time in a year. Almost inevitably, he got on the scoresheet, grabbing the equaliser in a 2-2 draw. It was a goal that extended Argentina's unbeaten run to 12 games, and confirmed them as one of the hot favourites to go all the way this summer.

At 33, this year's World Cup represents Batistuta's last realistic hope of major international honours. That is bound to make him even hungrier for goals than usual with England among Argentina's first opponents at the group stage. Ferdinand, Southgate et al. will have to be on their mettle when they come up against a man who has netted more than 170 goals in Serie A, a feat that has put him into the top ten all-time list of Italian goalscoring heroes.

Did You Know?

Batigol scored in 11 consecutive games for Fiorentina at the start of the 1994-95 season. It remains a Serie A record.

Gabriel Batistuta

Captain Marvel

England

Along with Michael Owen's wonder strike against Argentina, the enduring image from France '98 for England fans is David Beckham's petulant kick on Diego Simeone in the same match. If he had controlled his temper and England had finished the game with 11 men on the field, who knows what might have happened? The four years since then have seen an extraordinary transformation in Beckham's fortunes. From the villain of the piece who was on the receiving end of some of the worst abuse, Beckham has blossomed into an inspirational captain of his country. His artistry on the ball has never been in doubt; now, it is combined with a maturity which has seen him develop into England's new Captain Marvel. A Londoner by birth, Beckham made an early mark on the footballing world when he won an award at a Bobby Charlton Soccer Skills school. He had trials with his local club, Leyton Orient, and also attended Spurs' school of excellence. Manchester United then snapped him up as a trainee a couple of months after his 16th birthday. He became an integral part of the celebrated Old Trafford junior side which won the FA Youth Cup in 1993.

Beckham made his debut for United in a Rumbelows Cup match against Brighton in September 1992. But Alex Ferguson was careful to nurture his young star's development. Beckham had to wait until April 1995 for his first Premiership outing. The following season, 1995-96, he established himself as a first choice in United's midfield.

His rise to prominence came just too late for the Euro '96 party. Glenn Hoddle handed him his first senior international cap in September of that year, in a game against Moldova. It was in the opening Premiership fixture of that season that he scored one of the most spectacular goals ever. Seeing the Wimbledon 'keeper Neil Sullivan off his line, Beckham struck the ball superbly from some 60 yards out. Sullivan was beaten and Beckham had the Goal of the Season sewn up on the opening day.

He quickly developed into the best attacking midfielder in the country. A playmaker supreme, he sprays inch-perfect, defence splitting passes all over the field. He is acknowledged as the best crosser of a ball in world football. The wickedly curling balls he whips into the box are a defender's nightmare, but the kind of service that United's front men have thrived on. His dead-ball kicks are legendary, making corners and free-kicks a formidable weapon, both for United and England.

Beckham answered the critics who questioned his temperament when United met Inter Milan in the Champions League early in 1999. Less than a year on from the World Cup in France, it was billed as the return clash between Beckham and Simeone. Beckham rose to the occasion, gave a masterly performance in a 2-0 win for United and the two men shook hands and swapped shirts at the end of the game. United went on to a glorious treble, and Beckham's contribution was acknowledged when he was narrowly beaten by Rivaldo for the World Footballer of the Year award. That same year, Beckham married Victoria Adams Posh Spice and became a father for the first time. The family man off the field was showing increasing maturity on it. He helped United to win the Premiership in 1999-2000 and 2000-2001, while also being a pivotal player in the World Cup campaign, begun under Kevin Keegan's reign. Beckham's performances for his country, both under Keegan and Sven-Goran Eriksson, have even won over the boo boys of four years ago. Who can forget the climax of the game against Greece on October 6 last year, when Beckham's stunning free- kick in the dying seconds booked England's place in this year's finals?

David Beckham

Striking work-rate

Russian Federation

It is often said that it is a mistake for a player to return to a former club. Vladimir Beschastnykh seems to be one of the exceptions to that rule. The striker rose to prominence as a teenager at Spartak Moscow. His travels then took him to Germany and Spain, before he returned to the club where he first made his name.

Beschastnykh had only a handful of games under his belt when he hit two goals for Spartak against CSKA in the 1992 Russian Cup final. His international debut followed in August the same year, when he was just 18.After winning a back-to-back domestic championships with Spartak, Beschastnykh moved to Werder Bremen in 1994. Ten goals in his first season in the Bundesliga was a decent, if not spectacular return. His problems in Germany were off the pitch. Beschastnykh had struck up a good rapport with renowned coach Otto Rehhagel, the man who brought him to the club. When Rehhagel was replaced, the Russian striker became unsettled under the new regime. Matters came to a head and he was sold to Racing Santander in the summer of 1996.The first three seasons in Spain went well for Beschastnykh. He scored 26 goals during that period, and won over the fans with his pace, work-rate and ability to hold the ball up.

It all went sour during the 1999-2000 season, when he fell out with Santander coach Gustavo Benitez. He was dropped from the side, beginning a nightmare which lasted nearly two years. Things got so bad that Beschastnykh went on record as saying he even hoped the team would lose, in the hope that Benitez would be given the sack. That inflamed an already acrimonious situation. It seemed only a matter of time before he was shown the door. However, that took longer than both player and club expected. The issue was finally resolved last summer, when Santander released him on a free transfer - back to Spartak. Even as the move was being completed, Santander were being relegated from the Primera Liga , something which didn't upset Beschastnykh too much after the way he'd been treated.

The player said he was delighted to be back under the tutelage of Oleg Romantsev, the coach who had given him his first opportunity as a 17-year-old.Beschastnykh didn't let the difficulties he encountered in Spain affect his international form. When he lined up for Russia in the home match against Switzerland last October, he knew the team only needed a point to secure automatic qualification. A first half hat-trick put that beyond doubt. He scored from the spot after 40 minutes, then found the net with two headers before the break. Playmaker Igor Titov added a fourth in the second half.Beschastnykh has been part of Russian teams which have underperformed in recent years. He played in the side which went out at the first hurdle at both USA 94 and Euro 96. Russia didn't make it to France four years ago, nor to the finals of Euro 2000. Beschastnykh is keen to help his country improve on their poor recent record, starting in Japan and Korea this summer.

Vladimir Beschastnykh

Guile and trickery

Croatia

There are those who are in favour of the influx of expensive imports into the Premiership in recent years. Others are less happy. Alen Boksic is a player who crystallises that debate, and can be used as an example by both supporters and detractors of this phenomenon.

On the positive side, the Croatian is a marvellously talented player. In a Middlesbrough team not overly blessed with gifted individuals, Boksic stands out for his inventiveness and delightful touch. Any young player could learn a lot simply by watching him. On the negative side, it was widely trailed that Boksic moved to the Riverside in the deal worth more than £60,000 per week. His best days were behind him, some said. He was earning a small fortune in the twilight of his illustrious career. And far from helping talented youngsters to develop, some believe that Boksic and his ilk are hampering the progress of players from the youth ranks, and from the lower divisions.

Whatever side of the fence you come down on, Boksic's glittering career can't be questioned. He was a product of Hajduk Split's youth system, making his first-team debut when he was 17. That was in 1987. Four years later, he signed off from Hajduk by scoring the goal that beat Red Star Belgrade in Yugoslavia's domestic cup competition. Marseille was his next port of call. After a difficult first year, when there was a contractual wrangle over his transfer, Boksic began to show his quality. He helped the French club to win the domestic league and cup competitions, but his crowning moment came with a European win over AC Milan in 1993. He was France's top scorer that season, with 23 goals.

Marseille was then beset by a bribery scandal, and the club was forced to sell its young star. Lazio beat Juventus to win his signature. Three years later, after Euro '96, Juve finally got their man. Boksic spent just one year in Turin, however, before returning to Lazio. He helped the Rome club to win the Italian Cup and reach the 1998 UEFA Cup final, where they went down 3-0 to Inter Milan. Unfortunately, injury forced him to miss the World Cup finals in France. This year's competition surely affords 32-year-old Boksic his last realistic opportunity on the biggest international stage. It was the Boro striker who clinched Croatia's second successive appearance in the finals. He swept in a cross from Aston Villa's Bosko Balaban in Croatia's final group match against Belgium. It was the only goal of the game, and a vital one, for it meant that Croatia finished one point ahead of Belgium in the final group table.

Seven goals in 11 starts for Middlesbrough at the start of the current season showed that Boksic has lost none of his scoring prowess. He is injury-prone, however, and his work rate when the opposition is in possession isn't all it could be. Croatia still hasn't managed to replace its crop of ageing stars, of which Boksic is one, and the striker looks likely to lead his country's attack this summer. If he can steer clear of injuries, Boksic still has the guile and trickery to trouble the best defences in the world.

en Boksic

The young pretender

England

It is always hard for an exciting young player when he is compared to one of the greats of the past. When it's World Cup year and you've been dubbed "the new Bobby Moore", the hype and pressure can become excessive. Fortunately, Wes Brown is an unflappable, phlegmatic character and takes it all in his stride. In fact, those are some of the qualities which have prompted comparisons with England's World Cup winning captain of 1966. Brown also has all the hallmarks that made Moore such a great player. He is an excellent reader of the game, times his tackles to perfection and is totally at ease in possession. Add to that the fact that the United youngster is quicker than Moore was and better in the air, and it is easy to see why he is so highly regarded.

Brown was discovered playing in an under-12 game by United scout Harry McShane. McShane a former player himself and father of actor Ian had gone to watch Brown's brother play, but it was Wes's elegant, cultured performance that caught his eye, and United snapped him up for their junior ranks. Alex Ferguson gave his latest young prodigy his Premiership debut on the last day of the 1997-98 season. Arsenal had already clinched the Double and there was little riding on the game. Brown showed right from the word go that he had all the makings of a class defender.

He played 16 games the following season, the year of United's historic Treble. He didn't make the team to face Bayern Munich in the Champions League final, but there was some consolation as he won his first England cap under Kevin Keegan. With only 11 appearances in a United shirt to his name when he turned out against Hungary in 1999, Brown became the fastest-ever capped player.

A cruciate ligament injury sidelined Brown for the whole of the 1999-2000 season. Any fears that he wouldn't return the same player was soon allayed. This time it was Jaap Stam who was out for a long period, and it is a tribute to Brown that United didn't miss the player who had been such a rock at the back the previous year. Alex Ferguson's controversial decision to let Stam go last autumn must go down, at least in part, as a compliment to Brown. Laurent Blanc was bought as an immediate stop-gap, but Brown is obviously seen as the man with a long future ahead of him at Old Trafford.

Rio Ferdinand attracted all the headlines with his £18 million move from West Ham to Leeds just over a year ago. Given that benchmark, what Brown would fetch on the transfer market today is anybody's guess.

Did You Know?

The Man Utd fans cheer on Wes by singing "We've got Wesley Brown" to the tune of "Knees up Mother Brown".

Wes Brown

Brazil's captain

Brazil

Brazil played extravagant, stylish football at the 1982 and 1998 World Cups but lost. The team of 1994 didn't display the kind of flair associated with Brazilian sides but won. Brazil's longest-serving player and captain, Cafu, knows which he prefers. He was a substitute for the 1994 final. He came on early in a game which saw Brazil beat Italy on penalties after a drab, goalless 120 minutes of football. Four years later, Cafu was an automatic choice as the Brazil rollercoaster ran out of steam so dramatically in the final against France.

Cafu is a winner, and knows how vital it is for Brazil to be successful in big tournaments, almost at any cost. Not that he thinks his team will have to grind out a victory this summer. Cafu blithely believes that Brazil remains the best team in the world, despite the wobbles during qualification. He led the side to a very scratchy third place in the South America group. A string of defeats to some of the lesser lights including Ecuador and Paraguay also saw the country drop to third place in the FIFA rankings, behind France and Argentina. Cafu believes that the problem lay in the huge number of players used. When the best eleven is fielded regularly, he believes Brazil will be a match for anyone. In fact, Cafu is confident that, come June 30, he will become the fifth Brazilian captain to hold the World Cup aloft.

Even if his optimism for this summer proves unfounded, Cafu has still had an extraordinary career. Fifteen years ago, when he was a teenager just starting out in the game, Cafu was virtually dismissed as a player. He was turning out in midfield for Nacional, and wasn't thought to have the flair and creativity that such a position demands. His fortunes changed in 1989, following a move to Sao Paulo. There he came under the wing of the legendary Tele Santana, a former coach of the national team. Santana converted him into an attacking right-back, and for the past decade he has been just about the best in the business in that position. Five years at Sao Paulo brought Cafu a string of honours, including three Brazilian championships. In 1992 and 1993 he helped to Sao Paulo win the Copa Libertadores, the South American club championship. In 1994, the year in which he played his part in Brazil's World Cup win, he won the South American Player of the Year award. 1994 also saw Cafu gain his first taste of European football. He went to Real Zaragoza, but only for one year. That was enough for another medal, though. He played in the side which beat Arsenal in the 1995 European Cup Winners Cup final, the game decided by that famous 50-yard lob by Nayim which looped over David Seaman.

He then returned to South America for two years. His second sortie into Europe began in 1997. This time it was Roma and Serie A, where he has been ever since. The latest in a long list of credits came last summer, when he helped Roma win the Scudetto. Cafu may have turned 30 and have 100 caps to his name, but his desire remains undimmed. Although he plays at full-back, he is the embodiment of the old saying: the best form of defence is attack.

Did You Know?

Cafu's real name is Marcos Evangelista de Moraes. He was nicknamed "Cafu" after Cafuringa, a flying winger for Brazil during the 1970s

Cafu Marcos Evangelista de Moraes

The towering presence

England

In recent years, Sol Campbell's international career has provided him with welcome relief from the grind of playing in a Spurs side struggling to rise above mid-table mediocrity. He missed out on the 1991 FA Cup Final victory he didn't make his debut until the following year so the only success during his time as a first-team player was a Coca Cola Cup win over Leicester City in 1999. For a fiercely ambitious player such as Campbell, that was never going to be enough. His patience finally ran out when his contract ended at the end of last season.

The decision to move to Arsenal was a controversial one, but 27-year-old Campbell braved the taunts to become a key part of Arsene Wenger's rebuilding job in the Arsenal defence.

Campbell made his international debut in 1996, but came to prominence during France '98. He was a towering presence at the back in the last World Cup, and also made some eye-catching forays upfield. He thought he'd put England into the quarter-final when he powered in a header against Argentina, only for the goal to be ruled out for a foul by Shearer.

Euro 2000 was a different story. England were poor defensively, notably when they conceded three goals against Portugal after being 2-0 ahead. Campbell was given a torrid time by Luis Figo.

At the beginning of this season, Campbell took a while to adjust to his new north London home. A turning point came when he returned to White Hart Lane for the first time in an Arsenal shirt. He had an excellent game, despite being on the receiving end of some terrible abuse from the fans who once idolised him.

Despite such performances, Campbell is no longer a certainty for a place in an England starting XI. With the likes of Rio Ferdinand and Wes Brown maturing into excellent defenders, and Gareth Southgate still on the scene, competition is stiff. And although there may be an element of sour grapes, many Spurs fans think that Ledley King should also be ahead of Sol in the pecking order.

Did You Know

Sol's full name is Sulzeer Jeremiah Campbell.

Sol Campbell

Brazil

Stocky, speedy and explosive

The tactical importance of attacking full-backs in the modern game is widely acknowledged. It's a development which might have been made with Roberto Carlos in mind. He might not be the world's best defender, but with his rampaging forward runs, together with his explosive shooting, he tends to let the opposition worry about defending against him.

His attacking instincts stem from his teenage years in Brazil, when he played up front. Ironically, when he left Brazilian side Palmeiras to join Inter Milan in 1995, coach Roy Hodgson played him in midfield. Roberto Carlos wasn't happy there, and that may have been the reason why he spent just one season at the San Siro. Real Madrid paid £3 million to take him to Spain in the summer of 1996. Over the past six years he has been a fixture in one of the best sides in the world. He has two European Cup winners medals to his name, following Real's victory over Juventus in 1998, and Valencia two years later. In 1997, he was narrowly beaten by his compatriot Ronaldo for the FIFA World Player of the Year award. It was a terrific achievement, for the top individual honour in the game has regularly gone to the creative midfielders and top strikers.

The 1994 World Cup came a little too soon for Roberto Carlos. Branco, Leonardo and Cafu were all ahead of the talented 19-year-old in the pecking order; he thus missed out on Brazil's record-breaking fourth World Cup success. He was there four years later, though, when Brazil again looked like going all the way until the wheels came off in dramatic fashion in the final against France.

Along with David Beckham, Roberto Carlos is probably the best dead ball specialist in the business. Like the England captain, he practises tirelessly every day. Both players get incredible bend on the ball - a nightmare for goalkeepers and defenders. One notable difference is that Beckham likes to strike with the inside of the foot; Roberto Carlos, like so many Brazilians, prefers to get wicked spin and curl by using the outside of his trusty left boot.

Roberto Carlos will be 29 this year. Brazil's conveyor-belt of talent will surely throw up a new crop of young stars by 2006. For this stocky, speedy, explosive performer, Japan and Korea may be the last chance for World Cup glory.

Roberto Carlos

Mr Versatile

England

If you were looking for a nickname for Jamie Carragher, it would be difficult to choose between Mr Reliable and Mr Versatile. His level of consistency for Liverpool over the past couple of seasons has been of the highest order. Gerard Houllier has played him at full-back, as a central defender and in midfield, but he hasn't been fazed by being moved around. Carragher is a gritty, 100 percent player who gets on with the job he's given and never lets his manager or team-mates down. That said, he does prefer playing at the back. Last season, the Carragher Hyppia Henchoz Babbel defensive unit provided the foundation for Liverpool's glorious cup treble.

Sven-Goran Eriksson was quick to recognise the quality of Carragher's performances when he became England boss. He handed the player his first senior international start in last year's friendly against Holland. Carragher played in midfield that day, and although the game ended in defeat, Carragher confirmed his international credentials and has been a regular in the squad ever since.

Jamie was born in Bootle and joined Liverpool as a schoolboy. He quickly progressed through the junior sides, making his first-team debut at 18 in a Coca-Cola Cup semi-final against Middlesbrough. That was in January 1997. His first Premiership start followed in the same month and he celebrated the occasion - a home game against Aston Villa - by scoring in front of the Kop.

Carragher has been capped at Youth, Under-19 and Under-21 level. He captained the Under-21 side and holds the record for the number of appearances at that level. His first senior cap came as a substitute in a 1-1 draw against Hungary in April 1999. Three years on, he looks increasingly comfortable on the international stage.

Carragher is a rare and valuable commodity; a utility player who is also a top performer in all the positions he can play.

Jamie Carragher

The shot-stopper

Spain

Real Madrid have won the European Cup eight times, including two victories in the last four years. They are, arguably, the greatest club side of the post-war era. There have been periods when Real have accumulated huge debts yet they are always in the market for the world's best, and most expensive, players. The arrival of Luis Figo and, more recently, Zinedine Zidane, bears testimony to that.

Amid such glamour and affluence, the rise of their young goalkeeper Iker Casillas is a heartwarming story. Just two years ago, the teenage Casillas was turning up for training on public transport. The car park would be full of the most luxurious sports cars, owned by his team-mates, some of the most famous names in world football. Like Raul, he was just a local boy trying to make an impression. But Raul was by now one of those established superstars who overawed the youngster.

Within a year, this situation had changed dramatically. Casillas was Real's No. 1 goalkeeper, a member of the side which put out Bayern Munich and Manchester United on their way to the Champions League final, where they met Valencia. Casillas kept a clean sheet, Real scored three goals and he had a winner's medal for Europe's premier club competition. He was feted as the best young 'keeper in the world, and was soon an automatic choice for Spain.

Casillas is no Peter Schmeichel. Barely six feet tall, he isn't an intimidating physical presence who seems to fill the goal. But his great agility and lightning reflexes make him a terrific shot-stopper; time and again he has shown himself hard to beat, even in one-on-one situations.

He has come a long way since his boyhood days, when he drew the short straw of going in goal in kickabouts with his friends. Unlike most of his peers, Casillas found he enjoyed playing there. Then, in response to an advertisement by Real Madrid, Casillas turned up for trials for the Under-10 side. He has been at the Bernabeu ever since.

Casillas made Spain's squad for Euro 2000, but the 19-year-old didn't make it onto the pitch. Anyone who comes up against Spain in Japan and Korea will find they have to beat a superb young 'keeper if they want to progress in the tournament.

Iker Casillas

The inspiration and organiser

Paraguay's performances at the last World Cup kept everyone royally entertained. One of South America's lesser lights emerged from a very strong group at France '98. They finished second to Nigeria, and dumped Spain and Bulgaria out of the competition at the first hurdle. It took an extra-time "Golden Goal" from France's Laurent Blanc to end Paraguay's interest in the second round. Going out so narrowly to the eventual winners meant that the squad could return home with their heads held high.

Paraguay's star of France '98 in France was their portly goalkeeper Jose Luis Chilavert. This flamboyant character was and remains the talisman of the team. Like Fabien Barthez, he is rarely content to remain between the sticks. He likes to impose himself on the game by taking free kicks and penalties. One of his most recent spot kicks came in a volatile World Cup qualifier against arch-rivals Argentina last October. Chilavert slotted home to give Paraguay a 1-0 lead. It was his fourth goal in 16 games making him the team's second top scorer!

The game ended 2-2. It meant that Paraguay had lost their 100 percent home record. On the other hand, having also held Argentina to a draw in the reverse fixture, Paraguay were the only team that Argentina failed to beat in the fiercely competitive South America group.

Paraguay confirmed their passage to Japan and Korea before the final round of matches and, significantly, more comfortably than Brazil. Chilavert was again in the thick of the action when Paraguay met Brazil in an eventful match on the 15th August last year. Paraguay had already beaten the four-time World Cup winners 2-1 at home. Brazil's coach Luis Felipe Scolari, obviously worried at the number of points his team had already dropped, targeted Chilavert for some barbed taunts. He told his players to rain in plenty of long-range shots as the Paraguay 'keeper would be too old, too fat and too slow to save them.

The needle transferred on to the pitch, and insults were regularly traded between Chilavert and some of the Brazilian players, particularly Roberto Carlos. For the record, Chilavert was beaten twice - the game ended 2-0 to Brazil but the drama continued after the whistle as Chilavert got involved in a bout of fisticuffs with Roberto Carlos. The pair had to be separated by police.

Chilavert was the inspiration and organiser at France '98, when Paraguay conceded just two goals in four games. Now, they have some quality forwards to add to their resilient defence - one of them being Chilavert himself! Argentina and Brazil may be the two South American countries that most other sides will fear, yet Paraguay could be dark horses to go even further than they did four years ago.

Paraguay

Jose Luis Chilavert

Leading the line

England

Few strikers divide opinion more than Andy Cole. Wherever he's played Cole's goals-per-game record has been up there with the best. Yet the doubts have persisted. Glenn Hoddle famously got to the nub of the argument when he was England coach. Overlooking Cole for his France 98 squad, Hoddle said that he needed too many chances to score.

Cole's admirers - Alex ferguson included - have always been quick to spring to his defence. Graeme Souness is also a member of the fan club. He felt that his Blackburn side was missing a predator in the box, and was delighted when he prised Cole away from Old Trafford at the turn of the year to fill that role.

Cole began his career at Arsenal. He found opportunities at Highbury limited, a situation that wasn't helped by the fact that manager George Graham apparently rated Kevin Campbell a better prospect. He was sold to Bristol City in 1992 for just £500,000.

20 goals in 41 games at Ashton Gate was the kind of record that was bound to attract attention, and Kevin Keegan swooped to take him to Newcastle in March 1993.

Cole was soon hitting the net at a phenomenal rate for Newcastle, helping the team win promotion to the Premiership in his first season. The Toon Army has always revered the club's prolific No 9s, and Cole joined the pantheon of St James's greats which included Jackie Milburn and Malcolm Macdonald. No wonder, then, that there was anger and disbelief when Keegan agreed to sell him - and to Manchester United, of all teams. The £6 million that Newcastle received - £4.25 million more than the club paid for him - was no consolation to the die-hard Geordie fans. The goals and trophies came thick and fast in Cole's seven years at Old Trafford. His all-round game also improved markedly. He became very adept at holding the ball up and laying on chances for others, as well as getting on the scoresheet himself.

Cole's international fortunes looked to have improved when his old club boss, Kevin Keegan, replaced Hoddle in the England job. Keegan's reign was short-lived, though, as England got off to a shaky start in qualifying for the 2002 World Cup. Sven-Goran Eriksson came in with a clean slate, prepared to give each player his chance. Cole responded by finally breaking his international scoring duck, against Albania. It had taken 13 matches for him to get off the mark, hardly the kind of record to make the world sit up and take notice. But his rivals for a World Cup place - the likes of Fowler and Heskey - also have their critics. As the countdown to the tournament continues, it is still up for grabs as to who will get that striker's berth alongside Michael Owen. If Cole carries on at Blackburn where he left off at United, he will do his chances no harm at all.

Andrew Cole

England's classy defender

England

The phrase "meteoric rise" might have been invented for Ashley Cole. His progress from third choice left-back for Arsenal to international player has come at a dizzying speed. Perhaps he has been rather fortunate in that England are not blessed with too many left-sided defenders. However, Cole has pushed himself to the fore, both for club and country, with some classy performances over the past season and a half.

A product of Arsenal's Centre of Excellence, Cole started out as a striker. At 14, he filled in on the left-side of midfield in a junior game. By the time he'd progressed to the youth team, the move from attack to defence was complete as Cole established himself at left-back.

His old attacking instincts are there for all to see, though. He takes every opportunity to get forward, and his searing pace means that he can turn defence into attack very quickly, something which is very important in the modern game. There have been the occasional defensive lapses, and at 21 he is not yet the finished article. But where better to learn his trade than Highbury, home of the meanest defence of the past decade?

The latter part of the 1999-2000 season saw him out on loan at Crystal Palace, where he quickly became a favourite. When he returned to Highbury, Arsene Wenger obviously thought he was ready for Premiership action. First he allowed Nigel Winterburn to leave a player the young Cole had watched and admired greatly over the years. Then, early in the 2000-2001 season, an injury to Silvinho gave Cole an extended run in the side. He made an immediate impact and soon made the No. 3 shirt his own.

Cole soon had even more reason to pinch himself. In February 2001, with just a handful of Premiership games for Arsenal to his name, he was called up to the senior England squad by the new England manager. He didn't get on in the match, a friendly against Spain which England won 3-0. Michael Ball and Chris Powell each played 45 minutes at left-back that day. His debut came a month later, in the World Cup qualifier in Albania, and with every international game since he has cemented his place in the squad.

When Cole first arrived on the scene, many commentators noted that England could soon be fielding three players with the same surname. West Ham's Joe has yet to make his breakthrough, while Andy is struggling to get ahead of the Anfield trio in the pecking order of strikers. Of the three, Ashley is the one who looks most likely to feature in Japan and Korea.

Ashley Cole

Argentina's new star striker

Argentina

If the England players walk out onto the pitch to face Argentina on June 7th and find Gabriel Batistuta confined to the substitutes bench, there won't be too much cause for celebration. It will probably mean that they'll be facing Hernan Crespo, Argentina's new star striker, who has taken the place of Batigol in the national side over the past year or so. At 26, Crespo is some six years younger than Batistuta, yet he's been around long enough to establish himself as one of the most lethal finishers in world football.

Crespo was born in Buenos Aires. He made his name playing for River Plate, with whom he won the domestic championship in 1994 and 1995. Like so many of his compatriots he moved to Italy, Parma paying just £2 million for his services in 1996. He didn't win over the fans there immediately they were disappointed over the sale of folk-hero Gianfranco Zola to Chelsea the same year. After a slow start, Crespo found his scoring touch. He hit some vital goals in his debut season, helping Parma to the runners-up spot in Serie A.

He scored 62 goals in his four seasons at Parma, a record for the club. There was a UEFA Cup win in 1999, but eventually he sought pastures new where there was more chance of top honours. He joined Lazio in a players-plus-cash deal worth some £38 million, Parma having to console themselves with the huge profit they made on the player. Lazio were reigning Serie A champions at the time. The Rome side also included Juan Sebastian Veron, a great friend of Crespo who had also moved there from Parma. Crespo netted 26 goals for Lazio in his first season, making him Serie A's top marksman.

Crespo was sad to see Veron move on to Manchester United last summer, but the two will, of course, be reunited for World Cup duty. Crespo is likely to start up front, alongside Claudio Lopez, with Veron a potent attacking threat from midfield. Batistuta might not be too happy to play second fiddle to Crespo, but the latter's phenomenal scoring record of a goal every other game will almost certainly make him Argentina's number one choice in Japan and Korea.

Did You Know?

Hernan Crespo is an avid fan of the Rolling Stones.

Hernan Crespo

The star of Turin

Italy

Alessandro Del Piero first came to prominence after joining Juventus in 1993. He had been playing in the lower leagues up till then, while Roberto Baggio - whom he would later be compared with - was the big star at the Turin club.

In 1995, when he was still only 20, Del Piero inspired Juve to a league and cup double. Baggio was out with injury for much of the campaign, and Del Piero filled the boots of Italy's Golden Boy brilliantly. Juve nearly made it a glorious treble, as they reached the UEFA Cup Final in the same year. Their opponents were Parma, their main rivals for the Serie A title and the side they'd beaten to win the Coppa Italia. It proved to be one game too many, Juve going down 2-1 on aggregate.

Baggio was sold on to AC Milan, and Del Piero inherited his mantle as the young star of Italian and world football. Two more Serie A titles followed, and there was a European Cup victory over a star-studded Ajax side in 1996.

Del Piero's performances over the past nine years in the Italian league have not been matched when he has pulled on the blue shirt of the national team. In 1997-98, for example, he was in terrific form as he led Juve to the Scudetto; yet he had a very disappointing World Cup in France. It was a similar story two years later. Although Italy reached the final of Euro 2000, Del Piero himself was unimpressive.

A bad knee injury late in 1998 sidelined him for nearly a year. When he returned to action, he struggled for some time to regain his best form. Ironically, now that he is back to full fitness and performing well, he may find himself playing second fiddle to Francesco Totti. The Roma player has put himself ahead of Del Piero with some top-class displays over the past year. Even worse for Del Piero is the groundswell of opinion to restore Roberto Baggio to the national side. Now 34, Baggio has been in scintillating form with his present club, Brescia. When Italy were stuttering at 0-0 in their final World Cup qualification game, the crowd began to chant Baggio's name. Right on cue, Del Piero struck a stunning Beckham-like free kick, the goal which ensured Italy's passage to Japan and Korea. Still only 27, Del Piero might yet realize his potential on the world stage, and where better to start than this summer's global tournament?

Did You Know?

Alessandro Del Piero used to practise turning his garage light on and off - using a tennis ball.

Alessandro Del Piero

Latin magic

Ecuador

It is often said that there are no easy games in international football any more. The fact that Ecuador secured qualification to this summer's World Cup while mighty Brazil's attendance was still in the balance shows this to be true. For decades Ecuador had been the minnows of South American football, let alone the world game. Then, on the 7th November last year, they got the point they needed from their home match against Uruguay to take them to the finals for the first time.

Ecuador's hotshot during the gruelling 18-match qualifying series was Augustin Delgado, who was then playing his club football at Necaxa in Mexico. He hit nine goals in 16 games to take Ecuador to the brink of World Cup qualification. The fifth of those came in an historic 1-0 win over Brazil. His ninth came in Ecuador's stunning 5-1 away victory against Bolivia, ending the latter's unbeaten home record stretching back 16 years.

With a strike rate better than a goal every other game in a competitive cauldron such as South America, Delgado was bound to attract attention. Olympiakos was among the clubs reported to be interested in bringing him to Europe. Meanwhile, Necaxa tried desperately to fend off enquiries for their star player. It was only a matter of time before a deal was done, and Gordon Strachan emerged as the unlikely winner of the bidding war. Just as Ecuador were celebrating the historic moment which booked their passage to Japan and Korea, it was announced that Delgado would be joining Southampton in a £3.5 million deal.

Strachan has bought a player who can perform at the top level under intense pressure. He proved that last April, when Ecuador took on Paraguay in a dramatic World Cup qualifier. Ecuador went into the game full of confidence, having recorded wins over Chile, Venezuela and Brazil in their previous three outings. The run looked like ending in Quito, as they trailed Paraguay 1-0 and also had a man sent off. It was Delgado who saved the day. Just before half-time, he pounced on to a flick from Kaviedes and scored with a first-time shot. Eight minutes after the break, he hit what proved to be the winner. This time he showed his prowess in the air as he nodded home a cross from Mendez.

There is a long history of South American stars coming to top English clubs. Some have been great successes, others have flopped badly. Saints fans will soon find out which category Delgado falls into. As far as the World Cup is concerned, if he can maintain his present strike rate, Ecuador will be nobody's whipping boys.

Augustin Delgado

Brazil's flying winger

Brazil

Like his more illustrious compatriot Rivaldo, Denilson's genius lies in his left foot, while his right is mainly for show. Like Rivaldo, he had a very deprived upbringing in Brazil before arriving in Europe to make his mark on the world stage. But whereas Rivaldo was an instant success at PSV Eindhoven, Denilson initially struggled after joining Spanish side Real Betis. He was still only 20 when he made the move, following the last World Cup. He also found the £22 million price tag, a world record, something of a burden.

After some scintillating displays for Brazil, particularly at Le Tournoi in 1997, Betis naturally wanted to protect their investment. They tied Denilson into a long-term contract and inserted a buy-out clause that would scare off even the richest clubs in the world.

Things didn't go according to plan, however. Denilson failed to ignite Betis, scoring just five goals in two seasons. The low point was reached when the club was relegated to Spain's second division in 2000. It was announced shortly afterwards that Denilson would be going back to Brazil to join Flamengo in a loan deal. Details of the arrangement weren't released, but it was believed to involve Flamengo paying a fee in the region of £2 million, plus the player's salary. Some six months later, the deal fell through as Flamengo struggled to meet the payments. Denilson returned to help Betis in their bid for an immediate return to the Primera Liga. His form improved dramatically, promotion was duly won and Betis once again found themselves fending off enquiries for the player. Back in Spanish football's top flight this season, Denilson has continued where he left off. Once seen as a phenomenally expensive flop, Betis now want to build their side around him.

A flying winger is one of the best sights in football. The fact that he has at last come good is also great news for Brazil. Although he made his international debut in 1996, he was used mainly as a substitute at France '98. Unlike Ronaldo, who is still struggling with injury, Denilson is hitting form at just the right time. He could be the man to galvanise Brazil's campaign this summer.

Denilson Rezenda de Souza

Host's top young striker

South Korea

It could be a mistake to regard South Korea as sure-fire whipping boys this summer. They qualify this year as co-hosts, but it must be remembered that they have featured in every World Cup since 1986. Nor has the country been embarrassed in the past four tournaments. The South Koreans haven't managed to win a match yet, but there have been notable draws against the likes of Spain, Belgium, and Bulgaria; and in 1994 they only went down 3-2 to Germany.

Lee Dong Gook took part in France '98, when he was just 19. He is South Korea's top young striker, having notched eight goals in 18 games for his country. Six of those came in the Asian games in 2000. They helped fire South Korea to the third place play-off, where they faced China, another of this year's World Cup finalists. A tight encounter played in front of a 40,000-strong crowd it was Lee who scored the only goal of the game. It only earned South Korea third place in the competition, but at least he had the honour of finishing the tournament as top scorer. Given the ever-increasing competitiveness of Asian football, this was no mean achievement.

Lee is a bustling six footer whose main asset is his powerful shooting. He is also a quick-thinking striker. This is a crucial asset, as all coaches point out that when it comes to pace, the first two yards are in a player's brain, not his feet. Lee is a speed merchant on that score.

Lee has also recently done something all England strikers will be keen to do this summer score the winner against Nigeria. The dangerous African side went to South Korea to play back-to-back friendlies last September. The first of the games which was staged to celebrate the opening of the new World Cup stadium at Daejeon ended in a 2-2 draw. The teams met again a few days later. With the score at 1-1 in the dying seconds, Lee headed home Choi-Tae-Uk's cross to give South Korea a notable scalp.

Guus Hiddink, the former Holland coach, is the man charged with steering the South Korean side through their fifth successive World Cup campaign. In the run-up to the tournament, he was using the friendlies to find the all-important balance between youth and experience. In Lee he has both. And if Michael Owen or Emile Heskey can do what Lee did against Nigeria, it could just mean the difference between success and failure in the "Group of Death".

Lee Dong Gook

Poland's top-form 'keeper

Poland

In his relentless bid to close the gap on Manchester United and bid for the Premiership title, Liverpool boss Gerard Houllier highlighted the goalkeeping area as a cause for concern. Sander Westerveld was prone to too many errors. He made his last one at Bolton early this season, and Houllier made a double swoop into the transfer market. Chris Kirkland, the England Under 21 'keeper was prised from Coventry; he was the man for the future. There was an immediate need for experience between the posts, and Jerzy Dudek has filled that role brilliantly. Since his arrival, Dudek has been in excellent form and given an added resilience to Liverpool's defensive unit.

Dudek comes from Knurow, a mining town in Poland. Life for him looked like being the pits - quite literally. Football gave him an escape route. After four years playing semi-professionally, he finally got a contract with a league club, Sokol Tychy. He had barely unpacked his kit-bag there before he was snapped up by Feyenoord. Ed de Goey was on the books of the Rotterdam club at that time, but such was their confidence in their new signing that he was allowed to leave for Chelsea.

Feyenoord were regularly involved in the Champions League, giving Dudek a lot of experience of facing the best strikers in Europe. Liverpool have done no better than the Dutch club in recent seasons, but Dudek is convinced that Houllier is building a side with the potential to dominate Europe once again.

28-year-old Dudek is tall and agile, though he is no man-mountain; he doesn't fill the goal as some 'keepers seem to. The quality is there, though. As the halfway mark in the present season approached, he had played his part in helping Liverpool to the top of the table. His performance at Derby in early December was typical. Owen poached a goal early on and, with the team not playing well and under considerable pressure, Dudek produced a string of fine saves, including a penalty from Ravanelli. Three points from games like that is what championships are made of.

Dudek dreaded having to face a host of his team-mates in the run-up to the World Cup draw. That didn't happen, not for the group stage, at least. There is a fascinating history of England Poland World Cup clashes, however. Should they meet in the knockout phase this summer, Owen, Gerrard and co. will want to find Dudek in somewhat less impressive form than he has shown in his first few months at Anfield.

Jerzy Dudek

England

Cultured performer

When you pay a world record fee for a player, you might expect to be buying the finished article, not merely exciting potential. Yet when Rio Ferdinand moved from West Ham to Leeds for £18 million in November 2000, there were pundits who said he still had much to learn about the defender's art. A year on, most commentators now think David O'Leary got a bargain. Ferdinand has been hugely impressive for Leeds, so much so that the team has hardly missed Lucas Radebe, who has been missing through injury for much of the past year.

London-born Rio joined West Ham as a junior. Harry Redknapp promoted him to the first team at the age of 17, and his cultured performances were soon getting rave reviews. Along with Wes Brown at Manchester United, Ferdinand was being hailed as the future for England's central defence for the next decade.

In the modern game, where counter-attacking plays such an important part, it is a great advantage to have defenders who can get forward. Ferdinand has excellent ball skills; he is comfortable in possession, his distribution is extremely good and he is always a threat from set pieces.

Ferdinand's international call-up came against Cameroon in November 1997, when he had just turned 19. He made Glenn Hoddle's squad for France '98, and although he didn't feature in any of the games, it was experience which could only be of benefit. Surprisingly, Kevin Keegan omitted him from the squad which had such a disappointing Euro 2000. Japan and Korea 2002 thus represents the first opportunity for Ferdinand to show his worth on a big stage. Barring injury, he will certainly go into the tournament as first choice centre-back. It is a tribute to the way he has come on over the past year that the burning question seems to be: "Who should play alongside Ferdinand at the heart of England's defence?"

Did You Know

Rio and Les Ferdinand found out that they were cousins by accident; a chance meeting between some of their relatives revealed the family connection.

Rio Ferdinand

40 million pound superstar

Portugal

Luis Figo

Even in an age of hyper-inflation in football transfers, Luis Figo's move from Barcelona to Real Madrid in July 2000 was extraordinary. There was little change from £40 million when Real prised the 27-year-old Portuguese star from their arch-rivals in the Primera Liga. Eighteen months on, it looks to have been money well spent. Figo wasted no time settling in at his new club. He was in sparkling form as he helped Real to their first domestic championship in four years and reach the semi-finals of the Champions League.

His performances earned him the runners-up spot behind Zidane in the World Player of the Year awards. Their positions were reversed in the European Footballer of the Year honours, and many thought this is a truer reflection of the way the players had performed over the 2000-01 season. In December 2001 Figo was justly nominated World Footballer of the Year.

Figo came to prominence during Portugal's successive victories in the Under-20 World championship, in 1989 and 1991. Over the following five years at Sporting Lisbon, he developed the skills he is known for today: a quick brain and quick feet; wonderful balance and control; mazy dribbling with a very large box of tricks.

Whether playing as an orthodox winger or drifting inside and attacking the box, Figo was prolific both as a goal provider and goalscorer. It was only a matter of time before a bigger club snapped him up. Fittingly, the manager who came in for him was Barcelona's Johann Cruyff. The man who inherited Pele's mantle as world's best player in the 1970s no doubt saw much of himself in Figo: wonderfully stylish, devastatingly effective.

In five years at the Nou Camp Figo didn't disappoint. He was instrumental in bringing the club two domestic championships, two Spanish cups and the European Cup Winners Cup.

By 1996, Portugal's brilliant crop of youngsters with Figo the star ought to have matured into a side capable of taking the world by storm. They were dubbed "the Brazilians of Europe", yet could reach only the quarter-finals of Euro '96, and the semis at Euro 2000. The latter tournament provided a memorable clash with England, in which Figo starred - and scored as Portugal came back from 2-0 down to win 3-2.

Having failed to make it to France '98, Figo will be going all out for success this summer. At 29, he is at his peak and will be desperate for Portugal to finally realize their potential. Whatever the outcome in the World Cup, Figo has said he'd like to play in the Premiership one day. That will be some treat for the fans as long as he doesn't wait until his dazzling skills are on the wane.

Youngest international

South Africa

Quinton Fortune has been a bit-part player for Manchester United since he joined the club in August 1999. Like Solskjaer and Yorke, he has been a victim of the intense competition at Old Trafford. In Fortune's case, the fact that he is a left-sided midfield player - a position occupied by a certain Ryan Giggs hasn't helped as far as first-team opportunities are concerned. Of course, United are an exception. Fringe players at Old Trafford would be the first names on the teamsheet at most other clubs, and Fortune certainly falls into that category.

He was born in Cape Town on 21 May, 1977. He left South Africa at the age of 14, hoping he would be taken on by a European club. He caught Terry Venables' eye and had a spell in Spurs' junior ranks, but failed to establish himself. He moved on to Spain, first to Real Mallorca, then, in 1995, to Atletico Madrid. It was while playing for Atletico's B team that he came to the attention of South Africa's selectors. He became the country's youngest international when he turned out against Kenya in September 1996. He was 19 years 3 months old at the time. He went on to play in all three group matches as South Africa made its World Cup debut at France '98.

Fortune caught the eye of Alex Ferguson during the World Cup, and the United boss took him to Old Trafford the following summer, for a fee of £1.5 million. He made an early impact, notching four goals from six starts. He then joined up with the international squad for the 2000 African Nations Cup, where Bafana Bafana were knocked out by Nigeria in the semi-finals. The 2000-01 season was a stop-start affair for Fortune. Apart from the African Nations Cup, there were World Cup qualifying games, and he also played for his country at the Sydney Olympics. It meant that he was restricted to just seven outings for United as the club clinched yet another Premiership title. Unfortunately, his sporadic appearances meant that he missed out on a championship medal.

Towards the end of last season, it seemed that Fortune was on his way out of Old Trafford. He was said to be increasingly frustrated by a lack of regular first-team action, and Ferguson appeared ready to let him go. Serie A side Bologna was reported to be close to signing him, but Fortune made it known that he preferred to stay in the Premiership.

In the event, last summer came and went and no move materialised. Fortune has since knuckled down and concentrated on trying to impress when he gets the occasional outing. But as this experienced international approaches his 25th birthday, the issue is bound to resurface. There will be no shortage of interested parties the next time Fortune gets itchy feet.

As World Cup year got under way, Fortune was once again involved in South Africa's bid to win the African Nations Cup. This year's tournament, held in Mali between 19 January and 10 February, gave Fortune an excellent competitive warm-up before the big one in June. On the downside, it means missing several more games for United, which didn't help his first-team chances at Old Trafford.

Did You Know?

On the day Fortune was born, Manchester United beat Liverpool in the FA cup final.

Quinton Fortune

England's prize goal poacher

The early part of this season saw mounting speculation over Robbie Fowler's future. Even amongst the Anfield faithful, opinion was divided. One camp said his best days were behind him and Gerard Houllier ought to cash in while he could; the other maintained that he was still the best box player in the business, and was merely lacking confidence and sharpness through lack of opportunity. Houllier decided to take the money. It was a risk selling Fowler to one of Liverpool's main rivals for the championship, and it may yet rebound on the Anfield boss, for Fowler has looked back to his best since his £11 million move to Leeds.

Fowler is a striker's striker. In his nine years at the top Fowler has had his share of spectacular efforts fly into the net; but the poacher's goals bring him just as much pleasure. He knows that a tap-in and a 30-yard screamer go down on the scoresheet in exactly the same way.

Fowler opened his account for Liverpool in his very first game, a League Cup tie away to Fulham in September 1993. He followed it up by scoring all five in a 5-0 win in the return match at Anfield. He fired a highly creditable 18 goals in that debut season, but it was during the following three years that he hit top gear. He passed the 30-goal mark in each of those campaigns, firmly establishing himself as the natural successor to the great Ian Rush.

His scoring form earned him his first senior England cap in 1996. He made the squad for Euro '96, but Shearer and Sheringham were in such sparkling form that he only managed a brief substitute's appearance against Spain. He was also unlucky when France '98 came round, having sustained a bad knee injury in February of that year. Ironically, it happened in a match against Everton, the team he had supported a boy.

Despite his top-notch goal-scoring record, Fowler looked to be on his way out of Anfield at the beginning of last season. Both Gerard Houllier and Sven-Goran Eriksson seemed to regard the Heskey Owen partnership as the dream striking ticket. Fowler hit back with a terrific goal in the Worthington Cup final against Birmingham. He then came on as substitute in both the FA and UEFA Cup finals. He grabbed Liverpool's fourth goal in that memorable clash with Alaves. He signed off with two Premiership goals against Charlton which guaranteed Liverpool Champions League football this term.

Robbie Fowler

Nigeria's flying winger

Nigeria

After finishing fifth in the Premiership last season, Ipswich have suffered a backlash this term. As Christmas approached the Tractor Boys had just one league win to their name, a 3-1 home win over Derby. The man who hit two of the goals and gave a stunning performance on that August day was Finidi George, George Burley's £3 million summer signing from Real Mallorca. The Ipswich boss was left purring at George's performance. At last the side wouldn't have to rely so heavily on Marcus Stewart's goals.

Just as George was beginning to make a big impression on the Premiership, however, he suffered a fractured cheekbone in a 1-1 draw against Fulham at Craven Cottage. George had bravely contested a header with centre-back Alain Goma, and for his pains sustained an injury which kept him out of action for several weeks.

Like his international team-mate Kanu, George first came to prominence in the brilliant Ajax team of the early 1990s. He helped the Amsterdam side to a hat-trick of league titles, from 1994 to 1996, and played in the European Cup final of 1995, in which Ajax triumphed over AC Milan. He also has an Olympic gold medal, from Nigeria's victory in the 1996 Games.

George was part of a massive exodus from Ajax in the period following the European Cup success. He moved to Spain, where he spent five years, first at Real Betis, then with Real Mallorca. His one season at Mallorca wasn't his best, yet he helped them secure one of the four Champions League places awarded to the Primera Liga. The move to Portman Road meant that he missed out on the chance to play in Europe's premier competition, though Ipswich's qualification for the UEFA Cup was some consolation, and a factor in his decision to move to East Anglia. He returned from injury in time for Ipswich's visit to the San Siro in early December. The Tractor Boys went down 4-1 on the day 4-2 on aggregate leaving George to concentrate on helping lift the team off the bottom of the Premiership table.

30-year-old George has notched up nearly 50 caps for Nigeria since his debut in 1994. When he lines up against England this summer, the defenders on duty will have to be on their guard against this tricky winger who can cover 100 metres in under 11 seconds.

Did You Know?

Finidi George scored the goal that sent Nigeria to their first-ever World Cup, USA 94.

Finidi George

England's engine

Every top side has a driving force in midfield. Roy Keane fills that role superbly for Manchester United, as does Patrick Vieira for Arsenal. Unsurprisingly, Steven Gerrard is a big fan of both Keane and Vieira when he isn't doing battle with them on the pitch, that is. Gerrard has been a key player during Liverpool's recent resurgence and a vital cog in Sven-Goran Eriksson's exciting young England team. The fact that he's still just 21 suggests that he could become the best of this brilliant trio of midfielders. Dietmar Hamann thinks he already is, and he is well placed to judge. As well as playing alongside Gerrard for Liverpool, Hamann has also witnessed his trademark crunching tackles, raking passes and deft touches during England Germany clashes.

Gerrard is a Liverpool lad through and through. He joined the club as an eight-year-old and came through the junior ranks playing alongside Michael Owen. He made his debut 1998 and impressed more and more with each subsequent appearance. In some of those early games, competition for midfield places meant that he was played at full-back. With his pace, tenacious tackling and excellent reading of the game, he soon looked the part of an accomplished defender.

But his natural home is in midfield. It is in the engine room that his aggression, stamina and terrific range of passing come into their own. He is a classic box-to-box player, one minute nullifying an opposition attack, the next setting up a counter with a precision pass or bearing down on goal himself. When he gets within range, he can unleash a fearsome shot. Germany 'keeper Oliver Kahn found that out during that memorable encounter in Munich last September.

It was Kevin Keegan who handed Gerrard his senior international debut, against Ukraine in May 2000, in a warm-up game for Euro 2000. That tournament came a little too soon for Gerrard and he played just a cameo role in England's disappointing sojourn in Belgium and Holland. Now, just 18 months on, it would be unthinkable to leave a fit Steven Gerrard out of any England side. But fitness has been Gerrard's Achilles heel almost literally. A succession of niggling injuries have sidelined him all too often for Liverpool and Eriksson's liking over the past couple of years. If he can stay fit, the prospects are mouthwatering; how will the youngster who has taken the Premiership by storm measure up on the biggest stage of all?

Did You Know

31 May, 00 was a red-letter day for Steven Gerrard. He made his England debut, and was named in the squad for Euro 2000.

Steven Gerrard

England

Prodigious talent

After a dazzling Euro 2000, Nuno Gomes became the latest Portuguese star to join the exodus to a richer, more competitive European league. It was hardly a surprise. At 24, he had already spent three years each at Boavista and Benfica. Along with Sporting Lisbon and Porto, they make up the big guns of that country's domestic league. Gomes was thus running out of home-based options.

The lack of depth and the relative lack of resources in Portuguese football has been reflected in a dearth of success in European competition in recent years. Porto's European Cup win in 1987 was the last time a Portuguese team lifted a major trophy. Since then, Portugal has produced a crop of prodigiously talented players. Nearly all have outgrown the Portuguese league and gone on to bigger and better things abroad. Gomes was thus treading a well-worn path.

He joined Boavista in 1994, and won his first cap two years later. 1997 saw him move to Benfica. France '98 should have offered Gomes his first major opportunity to prove himself at world level, but Portugal crashed out in the qualifiers to maintain their reputation as perennial underachievers.Euro 2000 was Gomes's next big chance, and he grabbed it with both hands. Portugal's first game was against England, who went 2-0 after 20 minutes. Incredibly, Gomes scored the winner in the 60th minute, Figo and Pinto having brought Portugal level by half-time.

Gomes hit both goals in Portugal's 2-0 win over Turkey in the quarter-finals, and was also on target against France in the semis. Unfortunately for him, France ran out 2-1 winners, but he at least had the consolation of finishing joint-second top scorer on four goals, and left Holland and Belgium with a much enhanced reputation.

A £12 million move to Fiorentina followed almost immediately. Gomes went to Florence with a lot to live up to. He was filling the boots of Gabriel Batistuta, who had left for Roma. Gomes played down any comparisons. Lean and quick, his style was more akin to Filippo Inzaghi than the powerhouse "Batigol".Before his debut season was out, Gomes was facing an uncertain future at the club. The problem was off-field politics, not Gomes's performances on the pitch. Fatih Terim, the influential and charismatic coach who had brought Gomes to Florence, resigned abruptly in spring 2001. New coach Roberto Mancini wanted to rebuild, and Gomes was regarded as a prime saleable asset.

As the present season got under way, the situation remained unresolved. Gomes didn't allow the speculation about his future to upset his form, however. His performances for Fiorentina during the autumn of last year remained of a consistently high standard.

Playing for Portugal is bound to be something of a release from the club pressures that have built up over the past year. The World Cup might also be his chance to shine in the biggest shop window of all. Whether or not his club problems have been resolved by June, Gomes will be a dangerous customer, especially for central defenders lacking a yard of pace.

Portugal

Nuno Gomes

Gifted left-winger

Argentina

The last two seasons have been hugely successful for Valencia and one of their star players, Argentina's Kily Gonzalez. A technically gifted, tricky and aggressive left-winger, Gonzalez helped Valencia to successive appearances in the Champions League final. Along with Gaizka Mendieta, Gonzalez was outstanding in both campaigns, although both ended in disappointment at the final hurdle. In 2000, Valencia flopped badly in the final against Real Madrid; last year they went down on penalties to Bayern Munich.

This season, things haven't gone so well. Valencia didn't make one of the four Champions League places; renowned coach Hector Cuper departed for Inter Milan; and the club continued to haemorrhage players. In particular, the sale of Mendieta was a huge blow. He moved to Lazio, following in the footsteps of Claudio Lopez.

Gonzalez has been less than happy with the disruption of the past few months. No sooner had new coach Rafael Benitez taken charge than rumours of a rift began to surface. Benitez instigated changes, including in the sensitive area of players' diets. Gonzalez pointed out tartly that Valencia had managed to reach Europe's showpiece final two years running under the old regime. He felt the team hadn't done badly with paella and ice cream on the menu, and saw no reason to change.

Things weren't met much better on the pitch, either. Gonzalez reacted angrily after being substituted in a league match against Tenerife last November. He made his feelings known by shoving Benitez's arm as he left the field. He paid for the act of petulance a few days later, when he was left out of the squad that travelled to Glasgow for a UEFA Cup tie against Celtic.Gonzalez is clearly concerned that Valencia are not the force of the past couple of years. He has made no secret of the fact that he would like to follow Mendieta and move to Serie A. If he gets his dream move to Italy, it would bring to an end a six-year spell in Spain. He joined Real Zaragoza from Boca Juniors in 1996, and moved to his present club in 1999. It was no coincidence that he arrived at Valencia at the beginning of those two very successful years for the club.

Gonzalez will surely look on his World Cup duties with Argentina as a breath of fresh air after the recent upheaval he has encountered at club level. That could be bad news for the opposition. Strikers Batistuta, Crespo and Lopez will get close attention by any team Argentina meets - including England. But Kily Gonzalez remains one of the best left-sided midfield players in the world and will also need to be shackled by his opponents.

Kily Gonzalez

Man on a mission

Germany

Dietmar Hamann is a man on a mission. He has had and illustrious career at Bayern Munich and Liverpool - with an unhappy spell at Newcastle sandwiched in between. He has won a string of honours, including two Bundesliga championships, the German Cup and FA Cup. He has also joined a select group of players who have won a European trophy with two different clubs, having helped both Bayern and Liverpool to win the UEFA Cup. With Liverpool riding high in the Premiership and hot favourites to take the title this time, he may also soon have a domestic championship medal in two of the most competitive leagues in world football. Not to mention the fact that Liverpool are also still going strong in the Champions League.

Hamann's terrific career at club level has not been matched on the international stage in recent years. He was one of six Bayern players who went to France '98. Always excellent tournament performers, Germany surprised many when they bowed out at the quarter-final stage. Perhaps it shouldn't have been regarded as an upset to lose to a stylish Croatian side, but it isn't often that Germany finds itself on the receiving end of a 3-0 defeat.

If anyone doubted that Germany was in a transitional phase, then the country's dismal showing at Euro 2000 confirmed it. They will undoubtedly bounce back, and Hamann, who is nearly 29, will be keen for that to happen this summer.

It was Kenny Dalglish who introduced Hamann to the Premiership, paying £5.5 million to bring him from Munich to St James' Park at the start of the 1998-99 season. He spent just one year on Tyneside. Dalglish departed, and Hamann didn't hit it off with his successor Ruud Gullit. On the pitch it was an excellent year for Hamann, less so for the club. The statisticians who analyse all aspects of players' performances put him right up there with the very best midfielders in the country, a fine individual effort in a struggling side.

There was talk of a move to Highbury, but it was Gerard Houllier who got the German's signature. Hamann became Liverpool's seventh signing in the summer of 1999. The fee was £8 million; a great season at Newcastle had raised his price by a cool £2.5 million.

In the past two-and-a-half years he has been a dominant force in Liverpool's engine room. The axis he forms with Steven Gerrard is as formidable as any in the land - Anfield's heaving trophy room bears testament to that.

Hamann had to put aside club friendships twice during the World Cup qualifiers. He was smiling after the first encounter, when he scored the only goal of the game in Germany's 1-0 win at Wembley in October 2000. Things would be different a year later. Gerrard got the better of the midfield battle with his team-mate in England's stunning 5-1 win on German soil.

Did You Know?

Hamann's goal in Germany's win over England in the World Cup qualifying series was one for the record books: it was the last-ever goal scored at Wembley Stadium.

Dietmar Hamann

France's potent striker

France

Four years ago, 20-year-old Thierry Henry was preparing to play his part for France in the World Cup in the role of a flying winger. He ended the tournament as his country's top scorer, with three goals, and since then he has enhanced his reputation as one of the most potent strikers in the game.

Arsene Wenger must take a lot of credit for nurturing Henry's talents doubly so, for he has managed the player at two different club sides. Wenger first came across Henry as a teenager at Monaco. He recognised that the youngster had a dynamic combination of qualities: terrific ball skills and the kind of lightning pace that could have made him a top sprinter. Both men moved on, Henry to Juventus, Wenger to Japan. A year after Henry's World Cup exploits, in the summer of 1999, the two were reunited when Wenger paid £11 million to bring him to Highbury. Henry was replacing the prolific but temperamental Nicolas Anelka, whom the Arsenal boss had sold for more than £20 million. It was a typically shrewd piece of business as long as Henry could match Anelka's goal return.

Wenger's decision to play Henry as a central striker was a masterly one. Even the player himself was unsure about it; he didn't think his finishing was good enough. In the two-and-a-half years since, he has been a revelation in the role. Comparisons with Michael Owen have been inevitable, and Gooners fans naturally think that their man is no second fiddle to the Liverpool star, either in terms of pace or finishing ability.

Aime Jacquet left Henry out of the side which beat Brazil in the final of France '98, a decision which disappointed him bitterly. He is now vying for a place in the national side with the likes of David Trezuguet and his Arsenal team-mate Sylvain Wiltord.

Thierry Henry

Power and presence

England

Many eyebrows were raised when Gerard Houllier paid Leicester City a record £11 million to bring Emile Heskey to Anfield in March 2000. It was a lot to pay for a player who was nowhere near the finished article, and whose scoring record hardly made people sit up and take notice. Houllier knew he was buying sure-fire potential, and he wanted Liverpool to be the place where Heskey's prodigious talent blossomed. He had tracked Heskey's career over a considerable period and saw him as a vital acquisition in the rebuilding job he was undertaking at Anfield.

For 18 months, Houllier's team selection suggested that he felt the Heskey-Owen partnership offered the greatest promise, with Robbie Fowler and Jari Litmanen playing supporting roles. Heskey's power and physical presence was a perfect foil for Owen. And 22 goals in 2000-01 - his first full season at Liverpool represented an impressive goal return. At the end of that glorious year which yielded five trophies many Liverpool fans said that "Bruno" had made a bright start to his Anfield career, but had a long way to go to match the scoring feats of Robbie Fowler. Within a few months, Fowler was on his way to Leeds. It showed the confidence the club has in their young star that they were prepared to see a player of Fowler's stature leave.

Heskey went to the same school as another famous Leicester player who went on to bigger and better things with a Merseyside club - Gary Lineker. Heskey has already emulated Lineker's success at club level. Now, "Bruno" must be hoping that he can carve out the kind of international career that brought Lineker within a goal of equalling Bobby Charlton's all-time scoring record.

Kevin Keegan handed Heskey his first senior cap in February 2000, in a friendly against Argentina. He made two substitute appearances in Euro 2000. It is a testament to the strides he has made that he is now seen as a key member of Sven-Goran Eriksson's squad. Like Houllier, Eriksson seems to favour the Heskey Owen combination as his first choice strike partnership.

Heskey has achieved the first part of what he set out to do when he moved to Anfield: he has become a better player by having better quality players around him, and joined a side capable of winning trophies. This summer will be his sternest test yet, as he tries to impose himself on the best defenders in the world and help fire England to World Cup glory.

Did You Know?

Emile Heskey's middle name is Ivanhoe, his nickname is Bruno.

Emile Heskey

Italy's most prolific striker

Italy

As a youngster, Filippo Inzaghi was often pushed into playing in goal. All he wanted to do, however, was to score goals. His boyhood hero was Paolo Rossi, the man who fired Italy to World Cup victory in 1982. He found he had all the instincts of a striker to match his aspirations in that department, and he was soon banging in the goals in the lower leagues.

His first taste of Serie A football came with Parma. His brief spell at the club was plagued with injury and a move to Atalanta soon followed. Atalanta was a struggling side at the time, which made his 24-goal haul all the more remarkable. It earned him the Capocannoniere the coveted title awarded to the league's top striker. He attracted the interest of several big clubs, with Juventus winning the race for his signature. He joined the Turin club in June 1997, for a fee of £9 million.

Inzaghi hit 57 goals in his four-year spell at Juve. Towards the end of last season, he suffered a dip in form by his very high standards. David Trezeguet overtook him as the club's main striker, and Juve decided to cash in. He was still only 27, and Milan boss Fatih Terim paid £26 million to take him to the San Siro. This gave the mouth-watering prospect of a Shevchenko Inzaghi partnership, undoubtedly one of the most potent in world football.

Inzaghi's record as a marksman at international level is very impressive. Fifteen goals in 32 games makes him Italy's most prolific striker of the current era. When the amount of time he has actually spent on the pitch is calculated, it works out at better than a goal every other game, a fantastic strike rate.

The last World Cup was a personal disappointment for Inzaghi, as the national team coach at the time, Cesare Maldini, favoured Christian Vieri and Alessandro Del Piero up front. Giovanni Trappattoni is at the helm now, and "Superpippo", as he is known, will surely play a bigger part this time round.

Did You Know?

Filippo Inzaghi's younger brother Simone also plays in Serie A, for Lazio.

Filippo Inzaghi

Germany

The number one 'keeper

Franz Beckenbauer thinks that Oliver Kahn is the number one 'keeper in the world. UEFA agrees, having given the Bayern Munich player the Best Goalkeeper award three years in succession. And just to keep the theme running, he is also Germany's current Player of the Year.

The honours and plaudits aren't surprising, considering the role Kahn played in last year's Champions League final. He made three saves in the penalty shoot-out against Valencia. That alone was enough to make him the hero of the hour. The fact that he had single-handedly prevented Bayern from suffering the same last-gasp agony that Manchester United had inflicted on them in 1999 made his place in Germany's Hall of Fame all the more secure.

In saving Bayern from two Champions League final defeats, Kahn was responsible for subjecting Valencia to exactly that torment. The Spanish side had lost to Real Madrid the year before, and the players were distraught at another defeat. Kahn set aside his own elation for a moment to commiserate with Santiago Canizares, his opposite number in the Valencia side. It was a fine sporting gesture, one which brought him in yet another honour: UEFA's Fair Play award.

Kahn has been with Germany's top club side since 1994, joining them from Karlsruhe. The fee was £2 million, which remains a Bundesliga record for a goalkeeper. His trademarks are his powers of concentration, aggression and fierce will to win. His combative nature has given him his nickname: he was dubbed "Genghis Kahn" after a martial arts-style attack on Borussia Dortmund striker Heiko Herrlich during the 1999-2000 season. He puts himself through a gruelling training schedule, and it pays off in the extremely high level of consistency which he maintains.

Kahn won the UEFA Cup with Bayern in 1996, conceding just one goal in the two-legged final against Bordeaux. He has thus won all the major domestic and European club honours.

He made his international debut in 1995, but was second choice behind Andreas Kopke at Euro '96. That was Germany's last major triumph.

He was the undisputed number one by the time Euro 2000 came round. He conceded five goals in Germany's three group matches, including a Shearer goal in England's 1-0 win. It hardly mattered, as both sides were eliminated. He also conceded a rather more celebrated five goals last September - in just 90 minutes of glorious attacking play by England. Kahn is the consummate professional and dismisses that as an aberration.

Mick McCarthy's Republic side will be one of the first faced with the problem of scoring past Kahn this summer. Germany are not the force they once were, but while Kahn is there they will always be difficult to beat.

Oliver Kahn

Nigeria's enigmatic genius

Nigeria

The World Cup will throw up many clashes between club team-mates. In all three of England's group matches there will almost certainly be players who have to put aside friendships for 90 minutes. When Sven-Goran Eriksson's men face Nigeria, one of the most likely - and fascinating - confrontations will be between the Arsenal contingent on the pitch and Nwankwo Kanu.

As a player, Kanu is an enigma wrapped inside a riddle. In his four years at Highbury, he has entertained the crowds with his highly individual brand of magic. At 6ft 4in he can look ungainly, but he is also capable of some astonishing flashes of brilliance. It is usually a safe bet to expect the unexpected.

Kanu joined Ajax in 1993, when he was 18. At that time, the Amsterdam club was developing the best crop of young players in the world at its famed academy. Kanu wasn't overawed by rubbing shoulders with the likes of Kluivert, Davids and Seedorf. He helped Ajax to a hat-trick of domestic championships between 1994 and 1996. He also played a part in the 1995 European Cup Final, coming on as substitute in Ajax's 1-0 win over AC Milan.

In 1996, he helped Nigeria to take Olympic gold, and moved to Inter Milan the same year. It was shortly after he arrived in Italy that he was diagnosed with a heart valve problem. It not only threatened his career, but was also potentially fatal.

Kanu underwent corrective surgery, vowing to battle his way back to full fitness. It took him a year to achieve his goal. Unfortunately, by then he was the forgotten man at inter. The club was prepared to let him go, and Arsene Wenger stepped in with a £5 million bid which revitalised his career.

In his first two seasons at Highbury Kanu produced goals and entertainment in equal measure. In the last year or so, things haven't gone so well. He has often been the odd-man-out in Wenger's rotation system. The Arsenal boss has criticised him for under-performing; Kanu blames it on the fact that he hasn't played regularly enough. Rumours of a rift between the two have persisted. Matters weren't helped by Kanu's regular absences for international duty.

Despite his fall from favour and dip in form, Kanu will be a dangerous customer for England's defence. It will be hard to make preparations to shackle a player who is so extravagantly unpredictable. In fact, the only certainties will be the languid style, the loping stride and those enormous size 12 boots.

Nwankwo Kanu

Somersaulting to star quality

Ireland

Robbie Keane has packed a career's worth of transfer activity into his relatively brief time as a professional footballer. He has trodden a path travelled by quite a few players: performing brilliantly in the lower leagues, being snapped up by a top-flight club, having a spell abroad, then returning to the Premiership. What is remarkable is that Keane has done it all in just four years.

Not that the player has shown disloyalty to any of his clubs, or actively tried to cash in with these quick-fire moves. Quite simply, Keane loves to play and loves to score you only have to witness his trademark somersault goal celebration to see the enthusiasm he has for the game. If anything, he has been a victim of circumstance in the three high-profile transfers in which he has been involved.

Dublin-born Keane was the hottest property in Division One when he was 17. He was already established in the Wolves first team and was the club's top marksman in 1997-98. He had also made his debut for the Republic of Ireland.

A year later, Keane was ready to make the step up in class, and Wolves were ready to cash in their prize asset as long as the price was right. When a figure of £5 million was floated, Sir Alex Ferguson famously commented that the escalation in transfer fees had now reached a ludicrous level. The United boss said that £500,000 would be a more realistic figure for a player who would struggle to get into the reserve side at Old Trafford.

Not all clubs were put off. Aston Villa and Middlesbrough were very interested, but Coventry stumped up £6 million and Keane went to Highfield Road.

The young Irishman was outstanding on his Premiership debut. He hit two goals and left to the field to an ovation. Despite the impact he made, after just one season Coventry chose to double their money and let Keane go to Inter Milan. He quickly became a favourite with the Italian fans, and by December 2000, he was enjoying life in Serie A and felt he was improving as a player. Then, out of the blue, he found himself loaned out to Leeds for the rest of the season, with a view to a permanent deal. David O'Leary and the Leeds fans are the latest to wax lyrical over Keane's ability. The Viduka Keane partnership has regularly been O'Leary's favoured attacking option, though the acquisition of Robbie Fowler should make things interesting as Leeds push for the championship.

Mick McCarthy doesn't have the same embarrassment of riches up front, and Keane will be vital at the cutting edge of the Republic's World Cup dream.

Did You Know?

When he was a youngster playing for Crumlin, Robbie Keane passed up the chance to go to Anfield. He thought that his first-team opportunities would be better at Wolves.

Robbie Keane

Ireland's captain fantastic

Ireland

Captain Marvel is gone; long live Captain Fantastic. In a way, that sums up the last 20 years at Old Trafford. Bryan Robson was the driving force behind Manchester Utd in the 1980s; Roy Keane has assumed that role in the 1990s. The comparisons between the two players are obvious: a fierce competitive streak, tireless running, intense will to win, formidable leadership qualities. One important difference is that the side led by Keane has enjoyed an extraordinary run of success which has seen a mountain of silverware pile up in the Old Trafford trophy room.

It was Brian Clough who spotted Keane's potential when the youngster was turning out for Cobh Ramblers in the Irish league. A derisory £10,000 secured his move to the City Ground, where he quickly made a reputation for himself as a feisty sometimes over aggressive midfielder. In his three seasons at Forest the rough edges were smoothed out and he became the best young box-to-box midfielder around.

Alex Ferguson paid £3.75 million to bring Keane to Old Trafford in 1983, when he was a month short of his 22nd birthday. Now in his ninth year at the club, Keane has played alongside some wonderful artists on the ball, the likes of Giggs, Cantona and Beckham; yet it is he who makes United tick, and the team misses him more than anybody when he is not playing. It was no coincidence that the 1997-98 season, when Arsenal temporarily broke United's stranglehold on the Premiership, Keane was missing through injury for almost the entire campaign.

Keane is as fierce in his patriotism as he is in his tackling. He brings all his trademark skills to the Eire side, and, like Alex Ferguson, the Republic's boss Mick McCarthy pencils in Keane's name first, if he is fit. When the Republic had to face Iran in a World Cup play-off match last autumn, Keane had been out of the United side, struggling with injury. He turned out for the vital home leg, though, helping the side to build a winning platform to take to Iran.

Keane was on top form when the Republic went to the World Cup party in 1994. The team came through a very tough group and were not disgraced in going out to Holland in the second round. Having missed out at France '98, Keane, now 30, will want to put up a good fight in Japan and Korea. And the Republic will need him at his combative best if they are to make it to the knock-out stage for the third time in the last four World Cups.

Did You Know

In the last six seasons United have relinquished the Premiership title just once, in 1997-98. Roy Keane missed most of that campaign through injury. Coincidence?

Roy Keane

Sweden's goal machine

Sweden

For Celtic fans, December 6, 2001 is a landmark date. Not for their UEFA Cup defeat by Valencia - they'll want to erase that as quickly as possible. It marked the day when their goal machine Henrik Larsson missed what was by his standards an open goal. It came halfway through a nervy penalty shoot-out. Larsson bazed his spot kick over the bar and Celtic went on to lose 5-4.

When he was growing up in Helsingborg in the 1970s, the young football-mad Henrik was a big fan of the mighty Liverpool side, with Kevin Keegan his favourite player. His own development in the game was steady rather than spectacular. He came through the ranks of a Swedish third division side, then, at 21, joined joined Helsingborgs. After scoring 50 goals in two seasons, he was snapped up by Feyenoord for £300,000.

It was 1993 and the World Cup was looming. Once again, he didn't set Dutch football alight immediately, but impressed enough to make the Sweden squad for USA '94. Larsson was in and out of the side which had a great run up to the semi-finals. In the last four they lost to eventual winners Brazil by the odd goal, with Larsson back on the bench.

The next three years at Feyenoord were mixed. He eventually became unhappy at being played out of position and sought a transfer. Wim Jansen, the man who had signed him for Feyenoord, was now the Celtic boss and very keen to bring the striker to Parkhead. The deal was completed in July 1997, the fee just £650,000.

Larsson's 16 goals in his first campaign helped Celtic to the championship - breaking Rangers stranglehold of nine SPL titles in a row. He hit 39 goals the following season, although, ironically, Celtic finished that year empty-handed.

He began the 1999-2000 season in blistering form. Then, in a UEFA Cup tie against Lyon in October, he suffered an horrific broken leg. Incredibly, he recovered in time to play for Sweden at Euro 2000. The tournament didn't go well; Sweden finished bottom of their group. It was a huge disappointment for Larsson, particularly after Sweden had failed to make it to France '98. He did have the minor consolation of rounding Italy's keeper Francesco Toldo to score in the 2-1 defeat against the eventual finalists.

2000-2001 saw Larsson back to his very best. He banged in 53 goals to win Europe's Golden Boot award. Now that Valencia has ended Celtic's European ambitions for this season, Larsson is left to battle for domestic honours, then to try to get Sweden out of the Group of Death at the World Cup.

Did You Know?

Henrik Larsson has one of the more unusual goal celebrations: he pokes his tongue out.

Henrik Larsson

The exclusive Frenchman

France

Bixente Lizarazu was a member of the Bayern Munich side which won last year's Champions League final, a victory which helped put the agony of that last-minute defeat by Manchester United in 1999 behind them. This success earned Lizarazu membership of a very exclusive club. He was part of the France side which won the World Cup in 1998, then became champions of Europe two years later. By adding the premier honour at club level to victories in the two most important competitions in international football, he achieved a treble not seen for almost 30 years. The Bayern Munich side which ruled Europe in the mid-1970s contained several players - including the great Franz Beckenbauer who helped Germany to a European Nations Cup/World Cup double in 1972 and 1974. Lizarazu thus finds himself in exalted company.

In recent years, coaches have focused on the importance of having attacking full-backs. Along with Italy's veteran Paolo Maldini, Lizarazu is undoubtedly the best left-sided defender in the game. Like Maldini, he also loves to join the attack at every opportunity. In tight matches, players such as Lizarazu who can get forward and hurt the opposition in the final third of the pitch are a great asset.

Lizarazu joined Bayern Munich from Bordeaux, the only other club he has played for. He was a member of the Bordeaux side along with Zidane which reached the 1996 UEFA Cup final, where they came up against Bayern. The German side came out on top that day, though Lizarazu obviously impressed the victors enough to prompt them to take him to Munich.

Top footballers today live their lives under an intense spotlight. Lizarazu has an added pressure: he was born in the French part of the Basque region, and he has received threats from extremists who believe he denied his roots by opting to play for France.

ente Lizarazu

The Swedish 'fashion lion'

Sweden

The latest incarnation for Freddie Ljungberg's hair is a red tramline right down the middle. By the time the World Cup comes round, it will probably be all change for the man dubbed the "Fashion Lion in his native Sweden.

The hairstyle may have undergone many transformations, but there have been no such dramatic fluctuations in style on the pitch. He has been Arsenal's Mr Reliable in midfield in his three and a half years at Highbury.

His impact was immediate after arriving from part-timers Halmstads in a £3 million deal. He came on as substitute against Manchester United, and scored after less than five minutes on the pitch in a 3-0 win. He also showed what a competitive midfielder he is by picking up a yellow card.

If that was an impressive start, Arsene Wenger has praised his development since. Everyone pointed to the Vieira-Petit axis in the engine room as a key factor in Arsenal's Double season of 1997-98. It is high praise for the Sweden international that the midfield looks equally strong today.

In a single week last December, Ljungberg showed why Arsenal don't miss Petit. First, he scored at Portman Road in a Premiership match. He burst through the Ipswich defence like an express train, Thierry Henry played a perfectly-timed pass to match the perfectly-timed run, and Ljungberg slotted the ball past the advancing keeper. Four days later, he hit two more in Arsenal's Champions League win over Juventus at Highbury. The first was a true predator's goal, Ljungberg reacting first as Gianluigi Buffon spilled Vieira's shot. Late in the game, he lifted the ball beautifully over the world's most expensive 'keeper after a sublime piece of skill by Dennis Bergkamp. Midfield players who also have that happy knack of being able to get on the end of things in the box are a manager's dream. On that score, Ljungberg is up there with the best in the Premiership.

England will have to try and counter his all-action style and dangerous forward runs in the opening group match in June. It was his terrific display for Sweden against England in Stockholm in September 1998 that prompted Wenger to sign him. That was in a qualifying match for Euro 2000. Sweden, like England, performed poorly and went out of that competition at the first hurdle. It means that Ljungberg has no silverware to show for his considerable talents and efforts over the past four years. This born winner will surely collect a medal before long. Will it be with Arsenal, or will he help Sweden go a step further than their World Cup semi-final appearance of 1994?

Did You Know?

One of Freddie's last games for Sweden before he joined Arsenal was against Denmark. He scored past Peter Schmeichel. His debut for the Gunners was against Man Utd - and he scored past the Great Dane again.

Fredrik Ljungberg

Natural Flair

The huge influx of overseas players into the Premiership has been the subject of much comment in recent years. Over the same period traffic going in the opposite direction has pretty much dried up with the notable exception of Steve McManaman. Of the current crop of England players only McManaman and Owen Hargreaves are currently plying their trade on the Continent.

Playing in Europe has always been regarded as an important finishing school, where players can add an extra dimension to their game. Kevin Keegan, Gary Lineker and Paul Gascoigne all trod this path, with varying degrees of success. When 27-year-old McManaman decided he needed a fresh challenge in the summer of 1999, after 16 years at Liverpool, he chose to join Real Madrid. It was a free transfer under the Bosman ruling, and some Liverpool fans thought that McManaman had one eye on his lucrative move to Spain during his final months at Anfield.

Even at 29, McManaman continues to divide opinion among pundits and fans. Critics say he is a luxury player who has failed to reproduce his best club form when he has turned out for England. Macca fans point to his superb performances at Euro 96, where Terry Venables gave him a much freer role. McManaman is at his best when he is running at defenders at pace. He hasn't always been given the freedom to express himself; too often he has been played out on the left wing, with defensive duties too. That's when he has been least effective.

McManaman's career at Real looked to be over before it had really started when a new manager took over soon after he joined the club. Macca was told he had no future there, but he dug in and proved his worth. By the end of his debut season, not only had he forced his way into the first team, but also helped Real to reach the Champions League final. He capped it with a spectacular strike in the 3-0 win over Valencia. After nearly three years in the Primera Liga, where the technical and tactical side of the game is so advanced, McManaman is certainly a better all-round player. If he can combine the best of the Spanish game with the natural flair that made him such a favourite at Anfield, his best England days could still be ahead of him.

England

Steve McManaman

Italy's consummate professional

Paolo Maldini is not only a living legend, but a legend still performing at the highest level. His contract with AC Milan runs until the 2004-05 season, though he has confirmed that this year's World Cup will be his international swan song.

Maldini made his debut for Milan in January 1985, when he was just 16. Over the past 17 years he has won just about every honour in the game, including six Scudetti and three European Cups. He won the World Player of the Year award in 1994, the first defender to be so honoured. In the same year he helped Italy reach the World Cup final against Brazil, but finished on the losing side after a penalty shoot-out. That was the closest he's come to lifting the one trophy he would love to add to his haul before he retires. He had been in the side which lost to Argentina in the semis four years earlier; and he was there again at France '98 when Italy went out to eventual winners France at the quarter-final stage. England fans everywhere will sympathize with Maldini, for each of these World Cup exits was as a result of penalties. There was more disappointment for Maldini at Euro 2000, when Italy came within a minute of beating France in the final. This time it was David Trezeguet's Golden Goal which added to Madini's unfortunate record in major international competitions.

Despite so many agonising setbacks, Maldini's passion and hunger for the game remain as strong as ever. Even at 32, he trains with the enthusiasm of a junior.

Maldini has 500 Serie A appearances within his sights, an achievement that would put him into the top 10 on the all-time list in Italian football. He passed Dino Zoff's record of 112 international caps in October 2000, 12 years after making his debut in the famous blue shirt.

For someone who has been at the top of the game for so long, Maldini has maintained impeccable standards. He is a supreme defender, yet he also plays the game in the proper spirit. A wonderful footballer and consummate professional, his place among the all-time greats is already assured even if this summer ends in yet another disappointment.

Did You Know?

Paolo Maldini's father Cesare also played for AC Milan - then went on to coach the national team.

Italy

Paolo Maldini

Resilient last line

England

Almost inevitably, it was David Beckham's stunning last-gasp free-kick against Greece last October that grabbed all the headlines. It is the goal that carried England to the World Cup finals that will be replayed endlessly and live long in the memory. However, Nigel Martyn played an equally important part in saving quite literally England from having to go into the play-offs. He made two brilliant saves to prevent Greece from going two goals in front. He kept a side which was performing poorly, in the game, and effectively created the platform for Beckham to work his magic.

Martyn came back to earth in the next game. He spilled a shot that allowed Sweden to score in a game that finished 1-1. Fortunately, this time it was just a friendly, and many thought it a diplomatic result anyway, given the England coach's roots.

The next time these two sides meet it will be down to serious business. Will Martyn be between the sticks on that day? As the squad takes shape, the goalkeeping position looks to be one of the tightest calls. Although David James is staking a strong claim, it looks as though the two veterans Martyn and David Seaman will be battling for the jersey.

At 35, Martyn is the spring chicken of the two! But with goalkeepers, class and form have always been more crucial than age. Both are class acts, so it could come down to who the form player is in the run-up to the tournament.

Martyn signed for Leeds on the eve of his 30th birthday, in July 1996. The Cornishman had already enjoyed long and illustrious spells at Bristol Rovers and Crystal Palace. He had nearly 400 league appearances under his belt by the time he went to Elland Road. Having spent a long time learning his trade at these lesser lights of the footballing world, Martyn was desperate for top club honours and to unseat Seaman as England's established No. 1.

He started superbly at Leeds, winning the club's Player of the Year award in his debut season. It has been much the same story since, with the exception of the 2000-01 season, where he was out of action for a long period through injury. This season he looks as good as ever. His mature, commanding performances have given the defence confidence and authority. The young lions further upfield get a lot of the attention, but it is Martyn at the heart of a resilient defensive unit which has been just as important in the rise of David O'Leary's team.

Martyn cost Leeds £2.25 million, breaking the record held by David Seaman. Having spent so many years in the Arsenal man's shadow, Martyn would love to displace him again this time on the pitch at the World Cup.

Nigel Martyn

£30million star quality

Spain

At the beginning of this season, Gaizka Mendieta must have thought he'd made a timely decision to leave Valencia for Lazio. Having starred for the Valencia side which reached successive Champions League finals in 2000 and 2001, Mendieta relocated to Rome last summer. The £30 million move made him the most expensive Spanish player ever. It also gave him another crack at the Champions League. His former club had missed out on securing one of Spain's four places in this year's competition. Lazio were there, however, so Mendieta would have the chance to wipe out the memory of those two agonising defeats against Real Madrid and Bayern Munich in the last two finals.

But even as he was picking up his award as UEFA's midfield player of the year for his performances in last year's European competition, Mendieta was finding life tough at his new club. Lazio performed poorly in the first round of Champions League matches and were eliminated. The side was also languishing in the lower reaches of Serie A.

Nevertheless, Lazio have acquired a superb attacking midfield player. Mendieta covers acres of ground. He is a dangerous customer in the attacking third, and also does sterling defensive work a legacy of the fact that he started out as a full-back, albeit a not particularly impressive one.

Valencia had signed Mendieta as a 15-year-old. He was a very talented distance runner, too, and Valencia had a struggle on their hands to lure him away from athletics. He didn't set the world alight immediately. The early and mid-1990s was a very unsettled period at Valencia. A succession of managers came and went. They looked at Mendieta and played him in various positions. All too often, under pressure to produce instant results, they went into the transfer market, overlooking the gem of a player they already had on their books.

By 1997, Mendieta was at a low ebb, having failed to make a significant breakthrough. Then, Claudio Ranieri now boss at Chelsea came to the Spanish club. He liked what he saw in Mendieta's style of play and converted him into the playmaker he is today.

Mendieta made his debut for Spain in the qualifying matches for Euro 2000. He wasn't an automatic choice in Holland and Belgium, though. He was left out of Spain's opening match which they lost but transformed their fortunes against Slovenia and Yugoslavia. He scored from the spot against France in the quarter-finals. Spain were then awarded another penalty against the world champions late in the game, but Mendieta had been substituted by then. Raul missed with his kick, and Spain went out.

Mendieta certainly won't be a fringe player in Japan and Korea. He'll be central to Spain's hopes of transforming themselves from a highly talented collection of individuals into a powerful team unit.

Did You Know?

Mendieta made his debut for Spain in March 1999, in a 9-0 win over Austria. He scored his first international goal three months later, against San Marino. The final score? 9-0.

Gaizka Mendieta

The superstar of Asian football

Football is all about passion. Players of quite limited ability show their love for the game, week in and week out, on parks pitches up and down the country. It is quite surprising, therefore, to find a player at the pinnacle of the professional game who is said to have no deep, abiding love for football.

Japan's Hidetoshi Nakata is the superstar of Asian football. There are other players from the Far East who have gone abroad Arsenal's Inamoto and Portsmouth 'keeper Kawaguchi to name but two; but Nakata is undoubtedly the region's top footballing export. A star performer for Roma, he is the only Asian player to date to make the breakthrough into one of the major teams in a top European league.

Nakata's lack of emotion on the pitch is curiously double-edged: he neither goes overboard when his side celebrates a goal, nor does he react badly when things go against him. He simply gets on with the job that everyone agrees he does brilliantly, then goes home and forgets about football until he is next required to perform.

It was newly-promoted Perugia who brought Nakata from Japan's J-League to the rather more competitive Serie A in the summer of 1998. It took the slightly-built Nakata some time to adjust to the physical demands of Italian football. When he added power and strength to his existing skills, he proved to be a revelation. Roma boss Fabio Capello certainly thought so, for he parted with £15 million to bring him to the capital two years ago. That represented a £13 million profit in just 18 months for Perugia.

In 2000-01, Nakata's first full season at Roma, the club lifted the Scudetto. The fact that he has flourished in a team containing Francesco Totti is a testament to how highly he is rated. Both are playmakers, yet the two of them have been successfully accommodated within the side.

Nakata's strengths are his speed and an almost uncanny awareness of space. His ability to spot openings and find his team-mates with precision passes is something that Arsene Wenger, for one, is known to admire.

When the World Cup comes round, Nakata will inevitably revert to the role of a very big fish in a relatively small pond. He won't have the quality around him to be able to hurt the opposition with his creative play. As for the long-term future, other players are bound to follow the trail that he has blazed, and then Japan will be a force to be reckoned with.

Japan

...toshi Nakata

Style with power

Italy

Alessandro Nesta will always be remembered as the man who broke Paul Gascoigne's leg during a Lazio training session in 1994. Nesta was only 18, and had just made his Serie A debut for the Rome club he had joined as a boy. In fact, it was Gascoigne who made the tackle, though that was no comfort to Nesta, who was very upset by the incident.

Nesta's progress from that point on was sensational. By 1995, he was a regular in Lazio's first team, and he starred for the Italy Under-21 side which won the European Championship in 1996. On the strength of these performances he was drafted into the senior squad for Euro '96, though he didn't start in any of the games. He didn't have long to wait for his debut, though; that came against Moldova in October the same year.

France '98 should have been his first major international tournament, but a knee ligament injury sustained in a group match against Austria ended his involvement. Following a lengthy lay-off, Nesta returned to the side as captain. Lazio then enjoyed a very successful spell. The Italian cup went to Rome twice in three years, and in 2000, the coveted championship followed. It was Lazio's first Scudetto in 24 years. Nesta also captained the side to a special place in the record books as winners of the last-ever European Cup Winners Cup. Villa Park was the venue for this historic match, in which Lazio came out on top against Real Mallorca.

There were no injury problems at Euro 2000, and Nesta was finally able to show his worth in a major championship. Perhaps just as impressive is the fact that for the last two years he has been voted Best Defender in Serie A. Playing in a league which boasts some of the best exponents of the defender's art in world football, that is some accolade indeed.

Combining style with power, Nesta is regarded as the natural successor to Franco Baresi and Paolo Maldini in the pantheon of great Italian defenders.

Alessandro Nesta

Attacking full back

England

For those who believe in omens, the Neville Brothers are the first siblings to play for England since the days of Jack and Bobby Charlton. The latter pair both picked up World Cup winners medals in 1966, and England fans would love to see that achievement repeated in Japan and Korea this year. In truth, however, it is Gary, the older brother by two years, who is also the senior partner on the pitch. In recent years, he has proved himself to be the number one choice at right-back for Manchester United and England, while Phil has been more of a bit-part player in both camps.

Gary made his debut for United in 1994, when he was 19. Paul Parker was the established right-back at the time, both for United and England. Neville soon stepped into Parker's boots in both teams. His international call-up came in June 1995 against Japan. He had played just 19 first-team games at the time, a post-war record. For almost eight years he has been a key member of the side which has dominated domestic football, and his mantelpiece must be creaking under the weight of the medals he has won. Indeed, with a string of Premiership titles and FA Cup wins under his belt, not to mention that glorious European Champions League victory in 1999, there is little more for Neville to achieve at club level. He has already done more in the game than most players dream of, and with his 27th birthday coming up, he is only just approaching his prime.

As far as international football is concerned, Neville has much greater scope to build on his considerable achievements. He missed out on Euro '96, was part of Glenn Hoddle's squad which went out in the second round in France '98, and was involved in the disappointing Euro 2000 campaign. Getting to the latter stages of a World Cup must rank high among his remaining footballing ambitions. He is famously tight-lipped when the national anthem strikes up before an England match, but Neville is fiercely patriotic. He simply prefers to prepare for the big games in quiet contemplation.

Neville is not without his critics. His positional play in particular has been questioned, and there have been instances when he has been caught out with his hand raised, claiming for offsides that haven't been given. On the positive side, his understanding with David Beckham gives England a potent attacking option down the right flank, and the likes of Danny Mills and Jamie Carragher will have to play well if they want that England No.2 shirt.

Gary Neville

Footballer of the Year

England

Michael Owen turned 22 just before Christmas. He didn't quite manage to notch his landmark 100th goal for Liverpool in time for his birthday. A niggling injury kept him out of the side which went down 4-0 at Stamford Bridge, and he remained on 99 goals from just 181 games for the Reds. There was another very nice present, though: he was named European Footballer of the Year, following in the footsteps of Bobby Charlton, George Best and Kevin Keegan. Keegan had been the last English player to win the coveted award, back in 1979, when he was with SV Hamburg.

The award was no great surprise. Owen had had yet another year filled with electrifying performances, including the brace which snatched the FA Cup away from Arsenal, and that hat-trick in England's 5-1 win in Munich. This goal machine's resolutions for 2002 are simple: to help Liverpool win the league title, then get down to the business of the World Cup, the tournament which launched him to superstar status four years ago.

Owen's rise to the top came at the kind of pace that he himself is so noted for. He exploded onto the Premiership scene as a 17-year-old and began terrorising defences and plundering goals right from the word go. He scored on his debut, at Wimbledon on 6 May, 1997, and went on to net 30 goals in the next season, a haul which earned him the 1997-98 PFA Young Player of the Year award.

Owen was just 18 years 59 days when he was awarded his first senior cap for England. He became the youngest player this century to play for the national team, beating the record of one of the famous Manchester Utd Busby Babes, Duncan Edwards. Owen was 124 days younger than Edwards when he made his impressive debut in a friendly against Chile. Less than four months later, he also became the youngest player to score for England when he found the net in a World Cup warm-up match against Morocco.

It seems hard to imagine now, but Owen went into France '98 as a fringe player. When England fell behind to Romania in their second group match, Glenn Hoddle finally did what the pundits and public alike had been clamouring for. Owen hit the equaliser, and although Chelsea's Dan Petrescu scored an injury-time winner for Romania, Owen had assured himself of a place in the starting line-up. His blistering run and memorable strike in the match against Argentina then confirmed him as one of the stars of the tournament.

The Michael Owen of 2002 is a much better player than the raw talent of four years ago. His first touch has improved markedly, and he is now much stronger on his left foot and in the air. Which is great news for England, not so good for Argentina and the rest.

Michael Owen

The man with the Midas touch

France

For Manu Petit, 2002 is very unlikely to bring as many high points as the last World Cup year. Petit had the Midas touch back in 1997-98, his debut season for Arsenal. He played a key role in helping the Gunners wrest the Premiership title from arch-rivals Manchester United. An FA Cup win over Newcastle followed, and Petit was then part of the great French team which lifted the World Cup. He capped a fine tournament by grabbing the third goal in France's memorable 3-0 victory over Brazil in the final. Nor did the fairy-tale end there. That summer he dropped a coin into a Monte Carlo casino and promptly scooped a £17,000 jackpot!

It wasn't all smooth running for the player Arsene Wenger brought to Highbury from Monaco for £3.5 million in the summer of 1997. He struggled to adapt to life in England and the pressures of the Premiership, and came close to quitting Highbury after only a couple of months. Wenger knew Petit well, having managed Monaco when he was a young left-back there. The Arsenal boss succeeded in easing the player's worries, and he went from strength to strength as the season wore on.

Another crisis of confidence followed in the autumn of 1998. There was bound to be an anti-climax after the successes of the previous season; and some celebrated run-ins with referees didn't help. Once again Wenger smoothed things over, but 18 months later, the stylish midfielder finally decided to return to the Continent. After three seasons of consistently classy performances for Arsenal, Petit joined Barcelona.

Things didn't go well for him in Spain, however, and after just one season he was back in the Premiership with Chelsea. Claudio Ranieri had let Wise and Poyet go; Petit was drafted in, along with West Ham's promising Frank Lampard. The Frenchmen was soon turning in some top performances at the Bridge. The left foot is a sweet as ever, and even at 31, he continues to show why he is among the most accomplished midfield players in the world.

Did You Know?

Emmanuel Petit was France's Young Player of the Year in 1990, when he was an 18-year-old left-back at Monaco.

Emmanuel Petit

Quality on the left

France

When Marc Overmars and Manu Petit left Highbury and headed for Spain, Arsenal lost two players who had been hugely influential in their Double-winning year of 1997-98. Robert Pires was one of the players brought in to plug the gap, and at only £6 million, Arsene Wenger was spending a lot less than he'd raked in. For a club like Arsenal however, quality was always going to be more important than a bargain price tag. Could he cut the mustard on the left side of midfield the position Overmars had filled with such distinction?

Early reviews were mixed, as Pires took time to adjust to life in the Premiership. Silky running and close control are two of the most important weapons in his armoury. In the early games, he often found himself muscled off the ball. But the more games he played, the more impressive he looked, and by the end of last season operating in tandem with Ashley Cole he gave Arsenal great quality on the left flank.

Pires started his career at Metz, for whom he made his debut in 1993. In 1996, when he was 23, he won France's Young Player of the Year award. He made his international debut in the same year. He joined Marseille in 1998 in a £6 million deal, a French transfer record. He was there for just two years before Wenger made him the latest link in the French connection at Highbury.

Now 29, Pires is keen to get some medals for his mantelpiece. The Premiership and Champions League are the top priorities as far as club football is concerned. On the international front, stiff competition in midfield has meant that his opportunities have been limited. He was a fringe player at the last World Cup and Euro 2000, though he did get on as substitute in the final of the latter tournament. He had a hand in the Golden Goal which David Trezeguet scored to seal victory over Italy. Two years on, his form has made him much more likely to start on the pitch, not on the bench.

Robert Pires

Leading the line

Ireland

Niall Quinn is a fully paid-up member of football's "fine wine club" those players who have matured with age and are still producing vintage displays. Like Teddy Sheringham, who is also approaching his 36th birthday, Quinn continues to impress at the Stadium of Light. His partnership with Kevin Phillips remains one of the most formidable combinations in the domestic game. It may be a classic "little and large" partnership, but to label Quinn as the big target man who wins the ball for the more talented Phillips would be to do him a huge injustice. At six-foot four inches, Quinn is obviously a handful in the aerial battles, yet he is also capable of some very deft touches on the deck. Phillips is the first to pay tribute to his strike partner's flicks and lay-offs, which have helped him plunder so many goals over the past few seasons.

Quinn has really had two careers. He was at Arsenal as a teenager in the mid-1980s. In 1990, after five years at Highbury, he moved to Manchester City for £800,000. Peter Reid was a player at Maine Road at the time. The ex-Everton and England midfielder was then appointed manager, and had his first experience of seeing what Quinn brings to a side. Six years later, Quinn was nearly 30 and languishing in a struggling City side, when Reid, then at Sunderland, brought his former player to join him on Wearside. The fee was £1.3 million, which puts him in the bargain basement by today's standards.

Quinn had the honour of scoring the first-ever goal at the Stadium of Light ironically, in a 3-1 win over Manchester City. Sunderland had just won promotion to the Premiership, but it wasn't a happy experience, either for Quinn or the club. The genial Irishman missed most of the season through injury and Sunderland made an instant return to Division One.

Quinn scored twice in a dramatic play-off against Charlton at the and of the 1997-98 season, only to finish on the losing side. The following year they made no mistake. Quinn hit 21 goals as Sunderland won the 1998-99 Division One championship at a canter.

Three years on, the Mighty Quinn is still doing his stuff for Sunderland. He has pledged to end his career with the Mackems though when that will be is anybody's guess.

On the international front, Quinn holds a full set of caps for the Republic, having played at Schoolboy, Youth, Under-21 and Under-23 levels, as well as for the senior side. As at Sunderland, no one has yet managed to displace him. With the likes of Robbie Keane buzzing around him in the box, Quinn will give any World Cup opposition plenty to think about.

Did You Know?

Niall Quinn is horse mad. He already breeds them and has his own stables. He looks almost certain to go down the equine route when he finally hangs up his boots.

Niall Quinn

Outstanding at the back

South Africa

While Leeds have continued to make impressive strides over the past year, for Lucas Radebe it has been a period of frustration. United's captain and commanding central defender has been sidelined through injury for several months. It is the latest in a long series of setbacks for Radebe. He underwent surgery on both knees last season, and picked up another knee injury last summer as Leeds prepared for the current campaign.

If that wasn't bad enough, he was caught in the middle of the old club versus country debate. He was forced to make a late withdrawal from South Africa's squad to face Sweden last August, something which didn't please his international coach. David O'Leary, in his turn, has criticised South Africa for playing Radebe when he hasn't been 100 percent fit.

Having captained his country to their first World Cup finals in France four years ago, Radebe now faces a race against time to regain his fitness and his place in the Leeds side in order to stand a chance of making it to Japan and Korea.

Howard Wilkinson takes the credit for signing Radebe, who arrived from one of South Africa's top sides, Kaiser Chiefs, in September 1994. After a bedding in period, he developed into one of the most cultured defenders in the Premiership. When Leeds were nowhere near as good as side as they are today, Radebe was outstanding at the back. Tall, quick and an excellent reader of the game, he regularly shut some of the world's top strikers out of the game and made it all look quite effortless.

When George Graham inherited the side, he marked Radebe out as the key man in the rebuilding process. After David O'Leary took over 3 1/2 years ago, he too made it a priority to ensure that Radebe remained at Elland Road.

South Africa only returned to the international footballing fold in the early 1990s, in the post-apartheid era. Radebe was 23 when a new multi-racial side, known as Bafana Bafana, meant that South African football could once again be recognised by FIFA.

Radebe captained Bafana Bafana to victory in the African Nations Cup in 1996, and at the World Cup two years later. In 1998, they found themselves in the same group as France, to whom they lost 3-0. There followed creditable draws against Denmark and Saudi Arabia, but it wasn't enough for the team to progress to the second round.

Nearly 33, Radebe must regard this year's World Cup as his last realistic hope of appearing in the tournament. The ill-luck that has dogged him shows little sign of letting up, though. In his latest come-back match for the reserves just before Christmas, Radebe limped out with damaged ankle ligaments. Another three month lay-off was envisaged, putting his World Cup hopes in severe jeopardy.

Lucas Radebe

Spain's golden boy

Raul Gonzalez is the lynchpin of the Real Madrid team and the undisputed Golden Boy of Spanish football. Both titles have stuck with him in his eight years of top-flight football. Since his debut for Real - back in October 1994 Raul has seen a host of international stars come and go at the Bernabeu. Yet it is the local hero who is seen as the heartbeat of the team. As far as the Golden Boy tag is concerned, Raul is no longer the fresh-faced 17-year-old who became the youngest-ever player to take the field for Real; but he is still only 24, and no other rising star has come through to take his mantle from him.

In the modern era, it is unusual enough for a top player to remain faithful to one club for the best part of a decade. It is even more unusual when that allegiance is to a home-town club. Raul was born and bred in Madrid, although it was Real's great rivals in the city, Atletico, who first spotted his talents. He was the star of Atletico's youth side until the club made the extraordinary decision to disband the entire youth set-up. All the youngsters moved en bloc to the Bernabeu and Raul has been there ever since.

He was Real's top scorer with 19 goals from just 40 games in his first full season, 1995-96. He just missed out on the squad for Euro '96, making his international debut in October of that year, against the Czech Republic. It didn't take him along to open his account for his country; his first goal came in a 2-0 win over Yugoslavia in December 1996.

Raul's greatest successes to date have been for his club. He was one of the star players in the side that won the European Cup in 1998, beating Juventus in the final. That win ended a 22-year barren spell for the club. There was no such lengthy wait to repeat the success, as Real lifted the trophy again in 2000. It was a comprehensive 3-0 win over Valencia this time, Raul hitting the third to put him into double figures for the competiton. Two of his 10 goals had come in the quarter-final encounter with Manchester United at Old Trafford.

He was a member of the squad which went to France '98 and Euro 2000. His renowned leadership qualities at the Bernabeu didn't help much in either competition. Spain maintained their reputation as a group of highly gifted individuals who are perennial underachievers when the big tournaments come round.

Spain

Raul Raul Gonzalez

US midfield dynamo

6th December, 2001 was a day of mixed emotions for Claudio Reyna, the 28-year-old captain of the USA national side. He played for Rangers in their nailbiting penalty shoot-out victory over Paris Saint-Germain in the UEFA Cup. He was one of the heroes that sent half of Glasgow delirious; for the club would still be involved in European competition after the Christmas break, something that hadn't happened for eight years. Yet Reyna already knew he wouldn't be part of the new year adventure. His departure was widely trailed. He had been linked with a move to Sunderland for some time and it was confirmed on the morning following Rangers' win.

Commenting on his decision to head south, Reyna didn't surprise anybody when he cited the level of competition as the main reason. He wanted to pit himself against top quality opposition week in and week out; the SPL just didn't have enough depth.

Born in Livingston, New Jersey, this midfield general starred for his college side, and progressed through the USA's Under-16 and Under-20 sides. He was the youngest member of the American team that competed in the Barcelona Olympics in 1992. He would have repeated that feat at the World Cup two years later, but injury prevented him from being part of the USA's marvellous effort which saw them progress to the second round.

His failure to appear at USA '94 didn't stop Bayer Leverkusen from signing the 21-year-old. His opportunities at Leverkusen were limited, though, and he moved to newly-promoted Wolfsburg in a loan deal in July 1997. He spent a season and a half at Wolfsburg, where he established himself as one of the team's best players. His consistent performances were rewarded with the captain's armband making him the first American player to lead a European side.

Before that second season was over, Reyna found himself playing for Rangers. He broke into the team for the last six games of the 1998-99 season, in time to join the celebrations of Rangers' latest SPL championship.

In two and half seasons at Ibrox, Reyna proved himself a favourite with the fans. His tactical awareness, powerful running and versatility made him a valuable member of Dick Advocaat's team.

Reyna played in all of the USA's games at France '98. After their great success four years earlier, the States came back to earth with a bump, losing all three of their group matches. With more than 80 caps to his name, Reyna again looks likely to be the star performer who will be hampered by the lack of top quality around him.

Did You Know?

There is another international footballer in the Reyna household: Claudio's wife Danielle won 20 caps for the women's national team.

Claudio Reyna

The Brazilian genius

Brazil

It was a huge blow to Barcelona when World Footballer of the Year Ronaldo departed for Inter Milan in 1997. Not many signings would have assuaged the very demanding fans at the Nou Camp. Rivaldo was one of them. Barca bought out his contract at Deportivo La Coruna, where he had spent just one season since moving to Europe from his native Brazil.

Rivaldo had been brought up in impoverished circumstances. Now he was going to one of the most famous clubs in the world; it was a classic rags-to-riches story.

This wonderfully talented player with a lethal left foot had scored 21 goals for Deportivo, at just about a goal every other game. He went to on to hit 43 goals in his first two seasons at Barca, and with countless assists on top of that, he was a hugely influential figure in helping the side win back-to-back Primera Liga titles. It was on the strength of these brilliant performances that he won the World Footballer of the Year award in 1999.

It has been said that Barcelona have relied too heavily on Rivaldo's genius over the past four years. That has probably been even more the case since Luis Figo left to join Real Madrid. Barca have certainly underachieved in European cup competitions. In three out of the last four Champions League campaigns, Barca have been eliminated at the group stage. Last season, in the UEFA Cup, there was more disappointment as Liverpool knocked them out and went on to win the trophy. The two teams clashed again in the second round of this year's Champions League, and Rivaldo gave the Liverpool defence a torrid time as Barca ran out 3-1 winners.

First capped in 1993, Rivaldo played all seven games for Brazil on their way to the final of France '98. He found the net three times, but that was little consolation for the 3-0 defeat against France. Not surprisingly, he ranks this as his biggest disappointment in football to date.

Rivaldo will be looking to help Brazil go one better this year. He will have turned 30 by the time the competition kicks off, so it may well be his last chance to win the tournament. One thing is certain; he will use his right foot just to stand on as he always does and his left foot will be magic as it always is.

Did You Know?

The names of Rivaldo's son and daughter are inscribed on his football boots.

Rivaldo Vitor Barbosa Ferreira

The world's number one

Brazil

Along with UFOs and the Loch Ness monster, the performance of Ronaldo in the World Cup final of 1998 must go down as one of the great mysteries of the age. Everyone had expected Brazil's World Footballer of the Year to be the star of France '98, and four goals en route to the final merely confirmed that belief. The drama began when he was initially left off the team sheet to face France, then, at the last minute, he was included. He was said to have suffered a convulsive fit. There was also a suspicion that commercial pressures had been brought to bear in the decision to play him. Whatever the truth, he was clearly out of sorts on the day, a shadow of the player who had forged a reputation as the world's most feared striker.

Ronaldo was a goal machine from an early age. He scored heavily for Cruzeiro, the Brazilian side he played for in 1993-94. Even then, comparisons were being made with the great Pele. Ronaldo certainly matched Pele's achievement of appearing at the World Cup as a 17-year-old. However, while Pele took the 1958 tournament by storm, Ronaldo had to be content with squad membership at USA '94; he didn't feature in any of the games.

That same year he headed for Europe, and Bobby Robson's PSV Eindhoven. He hit 35 goals in his first season, enhancing his reputation still further. After just two years in Holland, Barcelona paid £13 million to take him to the Nou Camp. That year, 1996, he became World Footballer of the Year. He notched 34 goals in his first season at Barca, making him the Primera Liga's top marksman. He scored the goal which gave the Catalan club victory over Paris Saint-Germain in the European Cup Winners Cup final in 1997. He rounded off yet another fantastic season by once again picking up the World Footballer of the Year award, making it back-to-back titles.

Inter Milan broke the world record to acquire his services in 1997. Ronaldo didn't let the £18 million price tag worry him; he just carried on doing what he does best. He was on top form in Inter's victorious UEFA Cup campaign of 1997-98, though the team just missed out on the Serie A championship.

After years of unbroken success, the disappointments then began. Since the mysterious occurrences at France '98, Ronaldo has been dogged by injury. His most recent comeback after a more than eighteen-month lay-off during which his knee was reconstructed came in a UEFA Cup tie last September. He was soon back on the treatment table, this time with a thigh strain.

Fans everywhere will be hoping he can regain full fitness in time for the World Cup. Ronaldo in full flight is undoubtedly one of the greatest sights in football.

Did You Know?

Ronaldo has confirmed that a much-talked about clause in Brazil's contract with Nike does indeed exist. It states that he must play for his country at least once every two years.

Ronaldo Luiz Nazario da Lima

The elegant visionary

Manuel Rui Costa is one of that wonderfully talented crop of players that came through Portugal's ranks some 10 years ago. Luis Figo was one of his contemporaries when Portugal won the World Youth Championship FIFA's Under-20 tournament in 1991. Many of Portugal's stars have bemoaned the lack of depth in the domestic game, something which usually results in them eventually seeking a bigger club in a more competitive league. Rui Costa was at Benfica until 1994. It was then that the 22-year-old decided to move to Italy. Fiorentina paid £5 million to get their man, making him Serie A's most expensive newcomer that year. He went on to spend seven highly successful seasons at the club. During that time, he was the regular goal provider for Gabriel Batistuta; it was a potent partnership which lasted until the Argentinian left for Roma two years ago.

Rui Costa is a tall, elegant player, with great vision and a wonderful range of passing. Playing behind the main strikers, his main role is that of creator, although he gets his share of goals, too.

Last summer, he finally moved on. The new AC Milan boss Fatih Terim saw him as a pivotal player in a large-scale rebuilding process. At £28 million he wasn't cheap, but Terim knew what he was getting, having had a spell in charge at Fiorentina himself.

After almost eight years in Serie A, Rui Costa has just three cup medals to his name. For a league championship success he has to go all the way back to his Benfica days. His prospects of winning of the coveted Scudetto in the near future must be good: Terim has brought in Filippo Inzaghi and Andrei Shevchenko, two of the quickest and most exciting strikers in Italian football. Rui Costa is just the sort of player to deliver the killer passes which should see both forwards regularly in goals.

On the international front, he has been compared to Zidane, both in terms of the position he plays and the way he seems to act as a talisman for the team. When Rui Costa plays well, so do Portugal.

He was his country's best player at Euro '96 but the side only made it to the quarter-finals. He didn't get the opportunity to grace the last World Cup, as Portugal failed to qualify. He was in the side which was strongly fancied to go all the way in Euro 2000, only to fail at the semi-final hurdle at the hands of eventual winners France.

Most commentators agree that Portugal have the players to win a major tournament as long as the talented individuals can function as a unit. Nobody plays a greater part in linking the play than Rui Costa, so much will be resting on his shoulders this summer.

Portugal

Rui Costa

Strike force

Denmark

Ebbe Sand's footballing career began very late by modern standards. In an era when teenage sensations are becoming more of a normal than an exception, the fact that Sand didn't turn professional until he was 23 is quite remarkable. He chose to qualify as a building engineer first, though he won't be needing to deploy those skills for some while.

Sand's first league club was Brondby, where Peter Schmeichel launched his career. He was clearly a man in a hurry as he set about making up for lost time. And as a striker, that meant banging in a lot of goals. He hit an 11-minute hat-trick in November 1997, a Danish league record. He made it impossible for the selectors to leave him out of the squad for France 98 when he plundered 18 goals in just eight games.

Denmark emerged from the group stage along with France, and faced Nigeria in the second round. Sand came off the bench in that game to score after just 22 seconds, another record to add to an impressive curriculum vitae.

Denmark's World Cup hopes were ended by Brazil in the quarter-finals, but for Sand it had been a satisfying year. Apart from breaking into the national side, he had helped Brondby to a league and cup double, and been named Denmark's Player of the Year.

Sand's mercurial rise then received a massive blow when he was diagnosed with testicular cancer. He made such a remarkable recovery that a year later, in 1999, Bundesliga side FC Schalke 04 paid £4 million to take him to Germany.

Sand has proved to be just as prolific a goalscorer playing against much stiffer opposition over the past three years. Schalke are regularly having to give a "hands off" warning to other clubs. It is no wonder that they are desperate to keep him. Last season, his 22 goals nearly gave Schalke their first title in over 40 years. They were eventually pipped by Bayern Munich, though they did win the German Cup.

Sand's excellent performances were recognised by his fellow professionals, who voted him their Player of the Season. He edged into second place the great Oliver Kahn the man whose three saves in the Champions League Final penalty shoot-out gave Bayern victory over Valencia.

Sand's partnership with JonDal Tomasson will give Denmark a cutting edge to worry the very best defences this summer. They are very unlikely to finish goalless and pointless as they did at Euro 2000.

Ebbe Sand

Midfield jewel

England

Media-shy, unassuming Paul Scholes may go against the grain in modern football, where the top players are high-profile celebrities as well as athletes. Yet footballing insiders to a man regard him as a jewel of a player. As a classy midfielder with great vision and wonderful technique he is valuable enough. But Scholes also has that special knack for popping up in the box at the right time to score vital goals — a priceless quality.

Salford-born Scholes joined Manchester United as a 16-year-old. He was a member of United's famous Youth Cup-winning side of 1992, the team which spawned so many future stars. He made his Premiership debut in September 1994, against Ipswich Town, and wasted no time in making his mark, scoring both of United's goals in a 3-2 defeat. He finished his first season empty-handed, but since then the silverware has come thick and fast. Last season he picked up his fifth Premiership winners medal; he has also been part of two FA Cup-winning sides. Unfortunately, suspension forced him out of United's famous Champions League final victory over Bayern Munich in 1999.

His international debut came in 1997, against Italy in Le Tournoi de France. Once again, he soon opened his account, grabbing one of the goals in a 2-0 win. By the following summer, France '98, Scholes was an automatic choice for England. He started in all four of England's games and hit a terrific goal in England's 2-0 win against Tunisia.

A Euro 2000 qualifier against Poland provided Scholes with his greatest moment to date in international football. He grabbed a hat-trick in a 3-1 win and proudly marched off the pitch with the match ball tucked under his arm. Another qualifier in the same series brought his lowest point, when he was sent off in a 0-0 draw against Sweden at Wembley. Scholes is a classic fiery redhead, and there is always the chance that he will pick up the odd card.

When Kevin Keegan's team stuttered in the Euro 2000 qualifiers and had to face a volatile play-off match against Scotland, it was Scholes who made the difference. He scored both England goals in a 2-0 win at Hampden Park and effectively ended Scotland's hopes of reaching the finals.

Scholes started the all-important World Cup year with 13 goals from 38 England appearances, an excellent return for a midfielder. Even when he scores in the biggest games, Scholes' celebrations are typically understated. Cupping a hand to his ear as though straining to hear the fans' applause counts as a flamboyant display from this nuggety gem of a player.

Did You Know?

Paul Scholes became the first and last England player ever to be sent off at Wembley. His red card came in a Euro 2000 qualifier against Sweden. The game ended 0-0.

Paul Scholes

Wonderful balance

Germany

It is no mean achievement for a player to keep his place in a quality side over a ten-year period. Pressure from talented youngsters coming through the ranks is one limiting factor; another is the amount of money in the game, which tends to leave little room for loyalty between club and player, and vice versa.

Mehmet Scholl is a player who bucks this trend. This summer marks the 10th anniversary since he joined Bayern Munich. Over that period, some of the big guns from Italy and Spain have taken soundings, only to be given short shrift from the Bavarian club. The top men behind the scenes at Bayern include three of the greatest names in postwar German football: Franz Beckenbauer, Karl-Heinz Rummenigge and Uli Hoeness. All have been united in their determination to keep Scholl at the club.

The reason why Bayern have jealously guarded one of their prize assets is for the inventiveness and guile he displays in the final third of the pitch. He can play up front, but coach Ottmar Hitzfeld believes his best position is behind the strikers. Technically excellent and with wonderful balance, Scholl can turn games with an individual flash of skill. Mazy dribbles, deft flicks, clever free kicks: all are in Scholl's armoury, and he gets his share of goals, too.

Born in Germany of Turkish extraction, Scholl joined Bayern from Karlsruher at the start of the 1992-93 season. In the nine full domestic campaigns since, he has played 241 league games for Bayern and scored 70 goals. Of course, such statistics don't take into account the huge number of assists that have brought goals for his team mates.

Former national team coach Berti Vogts was one of the few men to have doubts about Scholl. He felt that Scholl drifted out of games too often and was rather lightweight when it came to the physical battles. Scholl worked even harder on his game and won Vogts over - not that it mattered, for the latter's days as national team boss were numbered.

The man in charge of these days is Rudi Voller, another former international star. As an ex-striker himself, Voller is a great admirer of the attacking threat that Scholl carries. When he is fit, Scholl's place in the side is no longer in doubt.Scholl has a string of club honours to his name, including a European Cup winners medal from Bayern's win over Valencia last year. He was part of the Germany squad that won Euro 96, but missed out on the less impressive World Cup campaign in France four years ago. He scored his country's only goal at Euro 2000, a brilliant effort which earned his side a 1-1 draw against Romania, Germany's only point of the tournament.

As a top-class left-sided midfield player, Scholl would solve Sven Goran Eriksson's problem on that flank at a stroke. As it is, Voller will have Scholl's flair and creativity at his disposal, while for Eriksson the search goes on.

Mehmet Scholl

England's veteran number one

David Seaman won't be far short of his 39th birthday when England head out to Japan and Korea this summer. The good news for England fans is that he is a mere stripling compared to some 'keepers who have graced the final stages of the World Cup. Peter Shilton had turned 40 when he played in the semi-final defeat by Germany at Italia '90; and the great Dino Zoff had also reached that milestone when he captained Italy to victory in Spain '82. Also, no one has yet done enough to wrest Seaman's England jersey from him. In fact, the battle for the goalkeeping spot looks likely to be between the Arsenal man and another veteran, Nigel Martyn.

Seaman's illustrious career began at Martyn's club, Leeds United. He moved on to Peterborough, but it was after he joined Birmingham City, in 1984, that he began to make a name for himself. When QPR came in for him in August 1986, they had to stump up £225,000, more than twice the amount the Blues had paid for him.

It was during his four-year stay at Loftus Road that Seaman made his England debut, in a 1-1 draw against Saudi Arabia in November 1988. Two years later, Arsenal made him the most expensive 'keeper in Britain when they paid £1.3 million to bring him to Highbury. Ironically, the man he replaced was John Lukic, who had been Leeds' No. 1 'keeper when Seaman was a young apprentice at Elland Road almost a decade earlier.

For nearly 12 years Seaman has been part of a defensive unit that has been the envy of the country. He has been a rock for England over the same period. Who can forget his penalty heroics against Scotland and Spain at Euro '96? Six years on, Richard Wright is threatening Seaman's Arsenal place. But the same was said of Alex Manninger, and the talented Austrian has departed, while the evergreen Seaman keeps rolling on. It would be a brave punter who would bet against Seaman being between the sticks for England this summer despite the rather dodgy pony-tail he sports these days.

Did You Know?

In 1990-91, David Seaman's first season at Highbury, he conceded just 18 league goals as Arsenal won the championship. Runners-up Liverpool had the second-best defensive record - and they let in 40.

David Seaman

Speed of mind

England

Who would bet against the evergreen Teddy Sheringham having an important role to play in the 2002 World Cup? He will have turned 36 by the time the England squad heads off to Japan and Korea, but as Sheringham fans point out: it doesn't matter if he's lost a yard of pace because he never had any to lose! Sheringham's speed is in his head. He sees situations very early, and has the touch to enable him to exploit those opportunities. In that respect, he is a lightning-quick operator on the pitch.

When Alan Shearer was the undisputed No. 1 striker for England, Sheringham was the perfect foil. Now, Michael Owen is England's top hitman, and the debate rages as to who would be his most effective partner up front. With his ability to drop deep and play his twin-striker in with deft flicks and slide-rule passes, Sheringham just might be the man.

Teddy was already the wrong side of 30 when Alex Ferguson brought him to Old Trafford to fill Eric Cantona's boots. He had had a long and successful career with Millwall, Notts Forest and Spurs; now he had the chance to win the top honours with the country's premier club.

With Cole and Yorke in superb form, he initially struggled to win a regular place. But he went on to play a vital part in the run-in to the glorious 1998-99 campaign. After helping United to secure yet another Premiership title, he came off the bench in the FA Cup Final to score one and make another for Scholes - a performance which won him the Man-of-the-Match award. Then, most dramatically of all, he came on as a late substitute in the European Cup Final against Bayern Munich and turned the game on its head. He scored one and laid on the winner for Solskjaer. After all those barren years, Teddy now had three winners medals on his mantelpiece within a matter of weeks.

1999-2000 was a season of restricted opportunities, and he was overlooked for England's Euro 2000 campaign. Last season, however, he bounced back in brilliant style. He scored 22 goals in all competitions and won both the Football Writers and the PFA Player of the Year awards.

Sven Goran Eriksson recognised Sheringham's terrific form by recalling him to the international squad for his first match in charge, against Spain in February 2001. He began the present campaign in the same rich vein, but now back at his beloved Tottenham. He was a substitute for that nervy clash with Greece last October, when England performed so poorly. Beckham got the plaudits, but Sheringham was also included in a very short roll of honour. He scored with a delightful header just seconds after joining the action, to make the score 1-1.

Sheringham may not start for England this summer, but his happy knack of coming off the bench to influence the outcome of games could be an excellent weapon in Eriksson's armoury.

Did You Know?

In January this year, Teddy Sheringham completed his 18th year in league football; he made his debut for Millwall in January 1984, when he was 17.

Teddy Sheringham

African power

Cameroon

In some ways, the footballing fortunes of Rigobert Song have mirrored that of his country. Cameroon lit up Italia '90 with their entertaining play. Led by the charismatic Roger Milla, Cameroon beat reigning champions Argentina in the opening match, then went all the way to the quarter-finals, where they went down 3-2 in a dramatic encounter with England. Cameroon then flopped at both USA '94 and France '98, finishing bottom of their group on each occasion.

It could be said that Cameroon's captain has also disappointed somewhat, after bursting onto the international scene as a teenager. After spells in France and Italy, Song's move to Anfield ought to have been the platform to really make his mark on the game. Perhaps he was unfortunate in that he joined Liverpool when the team was in the throes of a large-scale rebuilding process. He never really established himself, and it wasn't long before he was offloaded to West Ham. That could only be regarded as a backward step, as disappointing as Cameroon's performances in the last two World Cups.

Song went to Cameroon's elite youth academy. After a spell with one of the lower league teams, 15-year old Song joined Tonerre, the country's premier club. Two years later, when he was 17, Song became one of the youngest players ever to grace the World Cup finals. It was during Cameroon's warm-up matches for USA '94 that he launched his career in Europe. Cameroon prepared for the tournament in France, and an uncle of Song's took the opportunity to contact several French clubs on his nephew's behalf. Metz took him on, and weren't disappointed. There was also a spell in Italy before the dream move to Anfield.

Song learned his football on hard, bumpy pitches, where excellent control is a must. He also came through a system where football is still seen as an escape from deprivation, and is intensely competitive as a result. Song was not fazed by the Merseyside derbies he played in; he thought them quite tame in comparison with the domestic football of his homeland.

Both Song and Cameroon might be due for better things in 2002. Song has captained his country to victory in both the African Nations Cup and Olympic gold in Sydney. The strength of African football these days means that any team emerging as that continent's strongest must have a lot to offer.

It won't be difficult for Song to lead Cameroon to greater success than they enjoyed at the last two World Cups. Whether he can guide them to the dizzy heights of 1990 is another matter.

Rigobert Song

The cultured defender

England

Gareth Southgate is one of those unfortunate players who, no matter what they achieve in the game, will always be remembered for one dramatic moment of failure. His penalty shoot-out miss against Germany in the semi-final of Euro '96 hit all England fans hard. The team was on a roll and playing well; "Football's Coming Home" blared out from the stands; there was a widespread feeling that victory against the old enemy was on the cards. After his tamely-struck spot kick was saved, Southgate's face mirrored the disappointment of the country.

To his credit, Southgate went on to poke fun at himself by appearing in a celebrated pizza advertisement, where he was joined by other notable members of the "penalty missers club". It drew a good-humoured line under the incident, and showed that there is more to Gareth Southgate's game than one unfortunate error six years ago.

Watford-born Southgate made his name at Crystal Palace almost a decade ago, when he was the youngest captain in the Premiership. In 1995, Aston Villa paid £2.5 million to bring him to the Midlands. He had often played in midfield for Palace; it was at Villa that he established himself as one of the country's most cultured central defenders.

He was a key member of Glenn Hoddle's squad at France '98, and also featured in Euro 2000. Southgate was nearly 30 when he joined up with Kevin Keegan's squad for the latter tournament. When that adventure ended so disappointingly it seemed that his international days might be numbered. There was a crop of talented young defenders coming through, and it looked the right time to build for the future. Southgate's cause wasn't helped by the fact that he was also in dispute with Villa, a situation which culminated in his handing in a transfer request before the 2000-2001 season kicked off.

His £6.5 million move to Middlesbrough in July 2001 has given him a new lease of life, however. His performances have earned him a recall to the England squad, and he now looks to be a strong contender for a place in Sven-Goran Eriksson's starting XI when the serious World Cup business gets under way.

Gareth Southgate

Turkey's top striker

Turkey

As Turkey makes its first appearance in the World Cup finals since 1954, no man will be more important to the country's cause than Hakan Sukur. Sukur has been Turkey's foremost striker for a decade. He joined the country's best-known club side, Galatasaray, from Bursaspor in 1992. The goals immediately started to come thick and fast: 19 in the 1992-93 season, 16 the next, and 19 again in 1994-95. In between, he was a member of Turkey's gold medal-winning team at the 1993 Mediterranean Games.

It was only a matter of time before his goalscoring feats attracted the attention of clubs from some of the bigger European leagues. Torino paid £3 million to take him to Serie A in the summer of 1995. Sukur had just scored a spectacular goal for Turkey against Switzerland in a Euro '96 qualifier, and the Turin side was looking forward to a long and profitable association with its new star signing. Things didn't work out, however. He lasted just a couple of months and played only five games for Torino before returning to Galatasaray, for the same fee. Homesickness was said to have played a part, but there were also rumours that Torino was struggling to meet the financial obligations of the deal.

Sukur was not unduly worried. He was quite happy to go back to the club that was his first love. His only concern was whether Turkey's premier side could make the breakthrough and become the first team from the country to win a major European trophy. That dream was realised in 2000, when Gala beat Arsenal on penalties in the UEFA Cup final. On the international front, Sukur was part of a Turkey side which performed poorly at Euro '96. The country then continued its dismal run in World Cup qualifiers by failing to make it to France '98. Turkey did win through to the finals of Euro 2000, however, when Sukur was again widely regarded as being in the shop window. After a defeat by Italy and a goalless draw against Sweden, the Turks beat Belgium 2-0, with Sukur grabbing both goals. It was enough to see the team through to the quarter-finals, where they went down 2-0 to Portugal.

Sukur had impressed enough to earn himself another stint in Serie A. Inter Milan gave him his second chance to prove himself outside his home country. Unfortunately, this sojourn in Italy hasn't been a runaway success either. By last autumn, he was reported to be very unsettled, and was being linked with a number of clubs, including one or two from the Premiership. The man known as the Bull of the Bosphorus has a superb strike record at both club and international level. Now 30 and at his peak, Sukur is the man all Turkey's fans will be hoping can provide the firepower as that country embarks on its first World Cup adventure for 48 years.

Hakan Sukur

The unlikely hero

France

France looked up against it when they took on Croatia in the World Cup semi-final four years ago. Croatia had been in superb form throughout the tournament, and the French were further hampered by having Laurent Blanc sent off. With question marks over their strike potential already hanging over them, Les Bleus found an unlikely hero of the hour in Lilian Thuram. His brace of goals won the game for France and sent the home fans delirious. It was all the more remarkable because these were Thuram's first goals in 38 internationals. Since then, he has gone back into his goalscoring shell, concentrating on confirming his reputation as one of the world's top defenders.

Guadeloupe-born Thuram was a major part of a massive spending spree by Juventus last summer. He arrived from Parma, where he had proved that he was one of the most consistent performers in Serie A. Italian football has long been regarded as the natural home of the game's outstanding defenders. Not many imported players go to Italy and become as highly prized as the Italian stars in their own area of expertise. Baresi, Maldini, Costacurta, Nesta: these are some of the giants of Italian and world football over the past 20 years or so - all defenders. Thuram has proved himself worthy to enter Italy's Hall of Fame in that department. In fact, he has been nominated for the fiercely competitive Best Defender in Serie A award in each of the past two years. He was pipped for the honour on both occasions by Lazio's Alessandro Nesta.

Juventus didn't hesitate to pay £23 million to take the 29-year-old to Turin last summer. Juve are desperate to win the Scudetto, and their last Champions League success was back in 1996. For Thuram, club success is also a high priority. He has helped France to victory in the World Cup and European Championship, while a UEFA Cup victory with Parma in 1999 remains his only major honour to date at club level.

Lilian Thuram

Russia's playmaker

When it comes to attacking midfield players, Zinedine Zidane sets the standard all others are judged by. Any player who is compared to the former World Footballer of the Year must be some talent. Igor Titov has been dubbed the "Russian Zidane". The 25-year-old playmaker has been earning rave reviews for his performances for Spartak Moscow and Russia. He is playing in one of the less competitive European leagues, of course, but that could all change very soon. The predatory purchasers from the Bundesliga, Serie A and the Primera Liga are said to be circling their target, cheque-books at the ready.

Titov made his debut for Spartak as a teenager in 1995. Twelve appearances that year yielded just one goal. The progress he has made since then has been spectacular. By the time he was 20, Titov had established himself as the most influential player in the side. His goal return also improved markedly. Over the last three full seasons he has played 83 games for Spartak and scored 36 goals, a decent return for a striker, let alone a midfielder. For a player who is so creative and such a good finisher, Titov has a terrific work rate. He is no prima donna, content to stroll around the pitch and wait for the less talented work-horses to give him the ball. He has a great engine, and likes to roll up his sleeves and get stuck in to the physical battles that have to be fought in that area of the pitch.

Being an impressive physical as well as creative presence on the field has given rise to yet another comparison. Bayern Munich coach Ottmar Hitzfeld sees Titov as the perfect replacement for Steffan Effenberg when the latter decides to hang up his boots. Not only do the two share many qualities in their play, but both are inspirational leaders. Titov now captains the Spartak side, and Hitzfeld may well see him as the veteran Effenberg's eventual replacement in that role too.

Nominated as Russia's Player of the Year in 1998 and 2000, Titov finally won the award in 2001. Over the last year there has been a very close correlation between the fortunes of Titov and Spartak. When Titov has been missing from the side, or played when perhaps he shouldn't, Spartak's performances have dropped off dramatically. Conversely, when he is fit and firing on all cylinders, the team is transformed.

One big bonus for Titov is Vladimir Beschastnykh's return to Spartak. He now has a quality striker to link up with, and the pair will also form a dangerous attacking combination for Russia in the World Cup. Beschastnykh has already tried his luck abroad, in Germany and Spain, with mixed success. For Titov that test is still to come. A bidding war is expected any time now, and the winner can't hope for much change from £20 million. Not exactly a bargain basement price, but hardly a fortune for a player with the qualities of a Zidane or an Effenberg.

Russian Federation

Egor Titov

Denmark

Target man

Many football fans especially those who make up the Toon Army will feel that Jon Dahl Tomasson's name on Denmark's teamsheet must mean that the country is struggling for quality forwards. After all, Tomasson's time at St James' Park was hardly a raging success. But the signs are that he has put the year he spent on Tyneside well behind him and is rediscovering the form that made him such an exciting young prospect.

Copenhagen-born Tomasson left Denmark for Heerenveen in Holland when he was 19. After three successful seasons playing in the Dutch league, he joined Newcastle United, then managed by Kenny Dalglish. Tomasson was looking forward to playing off Alan Shearer and no doubt learning a lot from the England captain. Unfortunately, Shearer missed much of the campaign through injury. Dalglish frequently reshuffled his pack, including playing Tomasson in Shearer's role of target man. It went badly, and Tomasson suffered from lack of confidence and loss of form.

As Tomasson and Newcastle struggled, it was almost inevitable that the player would find his place in the national team under threat. The fact that he missed out on France 98 still rankles, and it is unlikely that Kenny Dalglish is on the Dane's Christmas card list.

Tomasson ended his Tyneside nightmare with a return to Holland. Feyenoord paid just £2 million for his services in June 1999, and he has spent the last two and half years showing what a ridiculously low valuation that was. Over that period he has been banging in the goals regularly for the Rotterdam club and for Denmark. At club level he has recently forged a powerful partnership with another "reject" from British football, Pierre Van Hoojidonk, who arrived from Benfica last summer.

On the international front, Tomasson put France '98 behind him by top scoring for Denmark on the road to Euro 2000. Unfortunately it all went wrong in the tournament itself. Denmark lost all three games, didn't score a single goal and finished bottom of their group. Tomasson and Denmark bounced back to qualify in fine style for this summer's tournament. Along with strike partner Ebbe Sand, Tomasson led the line as Denmark hit 22 goals to finish top of Group 3, ahead of the Czech Republic and Bulgaria.

Still only 25, Tomasson will be hoping his impressive form carries through to the finals. That will finally lay to rest the disappointment of France '98 and that frustrating season at St James' Park.

Jon Dahl Tomasson

Italy's golden boy

Italy

There is a great deal resting on Francesco Totti's shoulders at the moment. He is already having to live up to the tag of Italy's new Golden Boy, a burden that Roberto Baggio and Alessandro Del Piero have had to live with in recent years. Now, Italy boss Giovanni Trapattoni has named Totti as the key player in the Azzurri's World Cup campaign. He believes that the 25-year-old Roma star will have the same impact on the tournament that Zidane had four years ago. That is high praise, but also a lot to live up to.

Totti masterminded Roma's championship win last season, and started this year's campaign in the same vein. On the international front, he cemented his place in the Italy side at Euro 2000, and has grown in stature during the World Cup qualifying series.

For both club and country, Totti has been converted from being an out-and-out striker to playing in a slightly withdrawn role. Trapattoni and Roma boss Fabio Capello both feel that Totti's best position is playing just behind the strikers, where he can pull the strings as well as get on the scoresheet himself. All the play seems to go through him. The opposition can see that, but doing something about it is a different matter. Like all great players, Totti is able to find space even when defenders try to cut out the supply and shackle him.

He is certainly no overnight sensation, since he made his debut for Roma as long ago as 1993, when he was just 16. His talent was never in question, but he was hampered by the fact that Roma were in the shadow of Inter, AC Milan and Juventus. Juve's Del Piero in particular got most of the coverage and the plaudits. It wasn't until Euro 2000 that Totti really established himself. He regards that tournament as a turning point in his career. He gratefully accepted the compliments that were heaped on him afterwards, though he quickly pointed out that Italy finished second. He has since taken Roma to the top in Serie A; now he wants to the same for the Azzurri in Japan and Korea.

Did You Know?

Francesco Totti made his Serie A debut for Roma in 1993, when he was 16. Roma had snatched him from under rivals Lazio's nose three years earlier.

Francesco Totti

Frenchman on a hot-streak

France

France's World Cup victory four years ago was built on superb defence and inspirational midfield. The attack was the weak spot, and it was defenders and creative players who scored most of the vital goals.

David Trezeguet was one of several strikers tried during France '98. He played against Saudi Arabia during the group stage, and scored, but wasn't involved in the final. Two years later, when Euro 2000 came round, he still hadn't established himself in the team. Yet he popped up with the Golden Goal which beat Italy in the final.

Trezeguet's father must take a lot of credit for David's scoring touch. He used to take his son to matches and tell him to focus only on the movement of strikers.

Trezeguet started out at Paris Saint-Germain, but it was his time at Monaco, under Jean Tigana, that he regards as the most crucial in making him the player he is today. And that player is one of the hottest properties in Serie A. Juventus paid Monaco 171/2 million to bring him to Italy in the summer of 2000. His first season was something of a rollercoaster, a steep learning curve. But then he found top gear: he scored in five games on the trot at the back end of the season, and his hot streak continued into the present campaign.

Trezeguet's career has mirrored that of Thierry Henry in many ways. Both were talented 20-year-old fringe players at France '98; both learnt their trade at Monaco, then moved on to Juventus; and both are now regarded as among the world's top strikers. With France's defence and midfield still incredibly strong, they look an even more formidable outfit than the side that lifted the trophy four years ago.

David Trezeguet

Argentina's complete player

Argentina

There are some football pundits who feel that Juan Sebastian Veron has upset the balance of the Manchester United side since his arrival at Old Trafford. Alex Ferguson has had to shuffle his pack to accommodate the gifted Argentinian midfielder alongside Roy Keane and Paul Scholes, and it hasn't worked as well as United fans would have hoped.

When Veron arrived from Lazio in a £28 million deal last summer, it was universally acknowledged that United had done excellent business. A key player in Lazio's domestic league and cup double in 2000, Veron has been described as the most complete player in world football. Maradona was very impressed with the rising star when the two played together at Boca Juniors in 1996. Maradona was in the twilight of his career, while 21-year-old Veron was just beginning to make a name for himself as an attacking midfield player.

Italy beckoned, and Veron moved to Sven-Goran Eriksson's Sampdoria in 1996, making his international debut the same year. He was a top performer for the Genovese team, who weren't a high-flying side at the time. After Eriksson departed for Lazio, Sampdoria lost their star player, too. Parma was the next port of call, and Veron helped the side win the Coppa Italia and UEFA Cup. Alex Ferguson was reported to be showing interest in the player by this time, but it was to Rome where he headed next. Parma were, understandably, mortified to lose him after just one glorious season. At Lazio, where he was reunited with Sven-Goran Eriksson, he added the Serie A title to his medal tally something he'd just missed out on at Parma.

There were allegations concerning forged documents by which, it was claimed, Veron had entered Italy. He was cleared when the case went to court, but it obviously left a sour taste in the mouth and perhaps played a part in his decision to move to England after just two years in Rome.

Veron played in the Argentina side which eliminated England, then went out to Holland in the quarter-finals of France '98. He'll certainly line up against England again this summer and this time he'll face a team-mate or two. More interesting, perhaps, is the fact that he'll be trying to put one over on Sven-Goran Eriksson, the man who had admired his skills so much that he bought him on two separate occasions.

Did You Know?

One of Veron's heroes is Che Guevera. He has the name of the famous revolutionary tattooed on his arm.

Juan Veron

French driving force

France

Last October, Patrick Vieira came off the Stadium of Light pitch, annoyed with himself for having blazed a penalty over the bar. Sunderland boss Peter Reid was the first to offer his commiserations, and at the same time acclaimed the Frenchmen as the best midfield player in the world. He wouldn't get an argument from Arsenal fans. They know what fantastic protection he gives to the back four, snuffing out attacks before they reach the danger area. And when he is not winning the ball with those telescopic legs, he is driving forward at deceptive pace to link up with the forwards in the final third of the pitch.

Vieira was born in Senegal but brought up in France. His first club was Cannes, for whom he made his debut in 1993 as a 17-year-old. Two years later, he became the youngest captain of a French first division side, and also skippered France's Under-21 team. He joined AC Milan for £3.5 million in November 1995, but found his opportunities limited for the Serie A side. Arsene Wenger recognised Vieira's potential and began his reign at Arsenal by bringing the midfielder to Highbury in August 1996. The £3 million fee for a relatively unknown 20-year-old may have looked on the high side; five years on it must go down as one of the deals of the decade.

Vieira's midfield partnership with Emmanuel Petit was hugely influential during Arsenal's double-winning season of 1997-98. He then joined up with the national squad for their World Cup triumph on home soil. A substitute for the final, Vieira came on to set up Petit for the third goal which crowned France's great victory over Brazil.

Vieira's only weakness has been his disciplinary record. Opponents have cynically tried to exploit this by subjecting him to some extreme provocation. At one stage, a string of red and yellow cards threatened his future at Arsenal. Now he seems happier with life, and says he wants to remain at Highbury and captain the side one day.

Patrick Vieira

Italy's powerhouse striker

Italy

A much-travelled striker who once bore the burden of being the world's most expensive player, Christian Vieri has probably underachieved in the game up to now. Injuries haven't helped his cause, but even when fully fit he hasn't shown his best form with any degree of consistency.

Vieri was born in Bologna but brought up in Australia until he was 14. Moving back to Italy at that age was a huge culture shock and he was very unhappy for a time. Once he settled to his new surroundings, he became as passionate as a native-born Italian even if the tell-tale Australian accent is still there.

A big, powerful striker in the classic centre-forward mould, Vieri burst onto the scene as an 18-year-old with Torino. Between 1993 and 1999 he had six different clubs, spending just one season with each. Of those, he regards the year he spent with Juventus, 1996-97, as the most important in his career. He arrived at Turin as a 23-year-old who still had many rough edges as a striker. The coaches at Juve improved his game immeasurably, so much so that Atletico Madrid paid £12 million to take him to Spain.

His season at Madrid produced 24 goals, making him the club's top marksman. He fell out with the coach there, however, and Lazio brought him back to Italy in 1998, his goal tally in Spain having added £6 million to the price tag. Vieri was now enjoying his best period. At France '98 he was Italy's top scorer with five goals, one behind Croatia's Davor Suker, the tournament's overall hotshot.

After a season at Lazio, where he also finished as top scorer, Inter Milan made him the world's most expensive player. He began repaying the £31 million fee immediately, grabbing a hat-trick on his debut. After that blistering start, injury blighted the rest of the 1999-2000 season. It also meant that he missed out on Euro 2000.

Now 28, will be looking for a settled, injury-free run in the Inter side in the months leading up to the World Cup. Meanwhile, Italy fans will be hoping he can reproduce the sort of form that brought him five goals in five games in France four years ago.

Christian Vieri

The unpredictable Costa Rican

Costa Rica

Italia '90 is etched on the Tartan Army's collective memory as the year that Scotland lost 1-0 to Costa Rica. A week or so after the defeat, it suddenly didn't look so bad. Costa Rica also beat Sweden, and only went down by the odd goal to Brazil. Two wins was enough to take them through to the second round, where they finally succumbed to Czechoslovakia 4-1.

Costa Rica didn't make it to the next two World Cups, Mexico and the USA representing CONCACAF in both tournaments. Those two countries are there again this year, but they had to be content with the minor placings behind Costa Rica in the final Football Federation group.

Most British fans' knowledge of Costa Rican football begins and ends with Paulo Wanchope. This gangly 6ft 4in striker, who can be brilliant one game, and dire the next, has bemused the pundits as well as opposition defences over the past five years.

It was the spectacular side that was on view when he made his debut for Derby County, in March 1997. The Rams were at Old Trafford, which was far more of a fortress than it has been in recent months. Wanchope wasn't overawed, nor a respecter of reputations that day. He capped a fine performance with a stunning solo goal. Picking the ball up in a deep position, he simply ran at the heart of the United defence and slotted the ball home.

Over the ensuing months, his contribution fluctuated wildly, and Match of the Day pundit Alan Hansen, for one, could never quite make up his mind whether he was a class act or total clown.

Jim Smith had taken a £600,000 punt on the Costa Rican, after the latter had failed to impress in a trial at QPR. He hit 27 goals during his two seasons at Derby. In July 1999, Harry Redknapp paid £3.5 million to take him to Upton Park. The West Ham boss had recently bought Paolo Di Canio, and it offered an intriguing strike partnership. While the Italian was soon a revered figure in East London, Wanchope failed to spark.

Manchester City is the latest club to try and get the best out of this erratic performer. He frustrated former City boss Joe Royle and ended up on the transfer list. Kevin Keegan's arrival last summer brought him renewed hope of staying at Maine Road. He knuckled down at the start of the current campaign, scoring six goals in nine games and committing himself to helping City win an immediate return to the Premiership. He then suffered a knee injury which required surgery and kept him out of action for several weeks.

Wanchope will no doubt serve up the usual menu of eccentric skills and schoolboy errors in the World Cup. Defenders won't know what to expect from him, and that can only be to Costa Rica's advantage.

Paulo Wanchope

China's captain

China has a vast population and a passion for football. It is surely only a matter of time before the players make a big impact at some of the top clubs, and the country makes an impression at the major tournaments. As far as the latter is concerned, it is unlikely to be at this year's World Cup, the first for which China has qualified. But with the tournament based in Asia, China will have a great opportunity of making their mark in their debut appearance.

China's star player is captain Fan Zhiyi. He was one of the first of his countryman to blaze a trail into the more competitive leagues abroad, and it was an English side that snapped him up. Fan became the first Chinese footballer to play for an English league club when he signed for Crystal Palace in August 1998. Terry Venables was in charge of the Eagles at the time. He paid £1 million for Fan and another of China's top players, Sun Jihai. Sun found it difficult to settle, but Fan adapted well to Division One football.

In his three years at Selhurst Park, Fan proved to be one of the club's most consistent players. One thing he couldn't get away with in England, however, was to change his position quite so frequently. At his former club, Shanghai Shenhua, Fan's versatility together with the mediocrity of the league meant that he was able to play in every outfield position at one time or another, and still shine. That wasn't the case at Palace, although even here he turned out at the back and in midfield with equal comfort.

Fan played a key role in China's World Cup qualification matches. They were in a weak group - Oman, Qatar, Uzbekistan and the United Arab Emirates provided the opposition. Yet they did what every team tries to do; beat the opposition that was put in front of them.

As China celebrated, Fan was involved in a change of club. He fell out with manager Steve Bruce over the old club versus country chestnut. Bruce transfer-listed his sweeper after claiming Fan went back on an agreement to put club commitments before those of his country. Bruce himself then left the club, in acrimonious circumstances, but it was too late to save Fan's Crystal Palace career. Dundee United paid £350,000 to take the 31-year-old north of the border. Fan had long held the ambition to play in the Premiership. For now it is Scotland's premier league where he will ply his trade. No doubt his move will also mean his army of fans back home suddenly switching their allegiance from Palace to the Dens Park club.

China

Fan Zhiyi

France's midfield maestro

France

ZZ means just one thing in the footballing world: Zinedine Zidane, France's midfield maestro. This playmaker supreme is the man who pulls the strings for the reigning world champions. And with those memorable two headers against Brazil in the 1998 final, he showed that he is no slouch in front of goal, either.

The son of an Algerian immigrant, Zidane began his career with Cannes, whom he joined as a 16-year-old. It was after he moved to Bordeaux four years later, however, that he really began to build a reputation for himself. He made a stunning international debut in 1994, scoring two goals against the Czech Republic. He was soon being hailed as the new Michel Platini, the midfield general who crafted France's European championship win in 1984.

Zidane's first big chance to show whether such a comparison was justified came at Euro '96. It wasn't a success. He later claimed he was totally drained during that tournament, having had a gruelling season with Bordeaux, whom he had helped reach the UEFA Cup final.

The disappointment of Euro '96 was sweetened as he was made France's Player of the Year. A £3 million move to Juventus followed, and Serie A proved to be the perfect home for Zidane's artistry. He helped Juve win the Scudetto in 1997 and 1998, and the team also reached the Champions League final in both years. A famous double eluded the Turin side, though, as they were beaten by Borussia Dortmund and Real Madrid respectively.

Since then, the successes have come thick and fast. Following his stunning performances at France '98, he was made European Footballer of the Year. Two years later, there was another prestigious double as France added the European championship to their world crown, and Zidane received the highest individual honour the game can bestow: the World Footballer of the Year award.

Last summer he stunned Juventus with a transfer request. The Italian giants reluctantly agreed to let him go, and Real Madrid were happy to pay £48 million a world record for his marvellous skills.

Did You Know?

Howard Wilkinson once said that a combination of Zidane and his former France team-mate Didier Deschamps would create the perfect player. Zidane would be the skill merchant, while Deschamps - whom Eric Cantona famously dubbed "a water carrier" would be the work-horse.

edine Zidane

German pass master

Germany

Christian Ziege must be looking forward to spending more than a single season at a Premiership club. After an excellent year at Middlesbrough, followed by a frustrating one at Liverpool, Ziege is now enjoying life at White Hart Lane. A cultured left-sided wing-back or midfield player, Ziege is up there with Roberto Carlos as one of the world's best in that area of the field. He may not be quite as explosive a player as the Brazilian, but he is very classy on the ball and his passing is excellent. He also poses a great attacking threat with crosses whipped in from the left and from dead ball situations.

Ziege was born in Berlin, and began his footballing career as a goalkeeper. It was only after spells at local clubs Sudstern 08, TSV Rudow and Hertha Zehlendorf that he converted to an outfield player. With a move to mighty Bayern Munich, and from there to AC Milan, his career seemed to be on a steep upward curve. But things started going wrong during his time at the San Siro. Forced out of the side initially through injury, he found himself frozen out even after he had regained his fitness. His instincts were to stay, bide his time and wait for his chance. But it became increasingly clear that he didn't figure in Milan's plans. His club predicament was also affecting his international prospects. Ziege had made his debut for Germany in 1993 against Brazil, when he was 21. Now, when he ought to have been at his peak, he found that the club situation had put him out of the picture as far as the national team was concerned.

Bryan Robson had a turbulent time as Middlesbrough boss, but one of his great successes was securing Ziege's move from Milan to the Riverside in July 1999, for just £4 million. It was a deal which brought great mutual benefit. Middlesbrough had a top-quality international at a bargain price; Ziege had first-team football, renewed confidence and the chance to catch the eye of Germany's selectors once again. Ziege geared up for Euro 2000 with a hat-trick for Germany against Northern Ireland. His career seemed to be right back on track. Disappointment was just around the corner, however. First, Germany was dumped unceremoniously out of Euro 2000, finishing bottom of the group that included England. Then came a £5.5 million move to Anfield. All the signs were that it was a dream move. He was joining international team-mates Dietmar Hamann and Markus Babbel in a Liverpool side that looked to be going places. Liverpool was - but the place Ziege mostly found himself was on the bench, and sometimes he didn't even make the first-team squad. Injuries didn't help him get a settled run in the side, and when he did play, his form wasn't the best. As Jamie Carragher established himself as Gerard Houllier's first-choice left back, Ziege complained at the lack of opportunities he was being given.

A parting of the ways was inevitable. Ziege must have been relieved when Glenn Hoddle came in for him last July. Just as he enjoyed a new lease of life when he moved from Milan to Middlesbrough, so he is now much happier playing regularly in an improving Spurs side. The ups and downs of Ziege's footballing fortunes have been matched by those of the national team in recent years. Both could yet hit top gear in time for the World Cup, and embarrass those who believe Germany will be also-rans this time round.

Christian Ziege

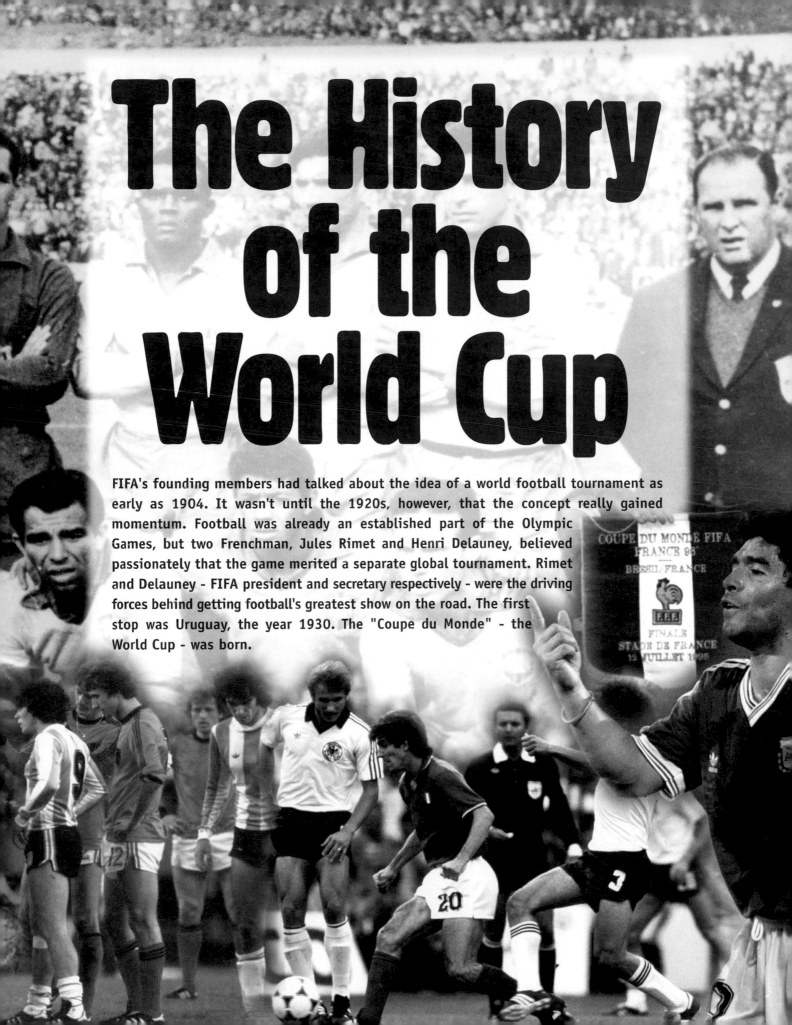

The History of the World Cup

FIFA's founding members had talked about the idea of a world football tournament as early as 1904. It wasn't until the 1920s, however, that the concept really gained momentum. Football was already an established part of the Olympic Games, but two Frenchman, Jules Rimet and Henri Delauney, believed passionately that the game merited a separate global tournament. Rimet and Delauney - FIFA president and secretary respectively - were the driving forces behind getting football's greatest show on the road. The first stop was Uruguay, the year 1930. The "Coupe du Monde" - the World Cup - was born.

1930 Uruguay

Uruguay 4 Argentina 2

Thirteen teams compete first World Cup

The early tournaments were blighted by political shenanigans and ill feeling. Uruguay was awarded the inaugural competition after promising a new stadium and free travel and accommodation for the participants. Six South American countries agreed to compete, together with Mexico and the USA. But European countries were reluctant to commit themselves to a three-week sea journey, even if the Uruguayan authorities were picking up the bill. As far as the home nations were concerned, the journey wasn't the problem. All four countries had walked out of FIFA over the hotly-disputed issue of broken-time payments. These were payments made to players to make up their wages when they took time off to play football. England, Scotland, Ireland and Wales had fiercely opposed such payments, trying to preserve the integrity of true amateur status. FIFA, on the other hand, embraced the beginnings of professionalism. This drawn out dispute meant that none of the home countries featured in any of the first three World Cups.

The Olympic finalists

There was European representation in Uruguay, however. At the last minute, France, Yugoslavia, Romania and Belgium relented and a 13-strong competition got under way.

Argentina, Yugoslavia and the USA, together with host country Uruguay, emerged as winners of the four mini-groups and went forward to the semi-finals. Argentina thumped the USA 6-1 to cruise through to the final, where they were joined by Uruguay, who beat Yugoslavia by the same score. The final, which took place at the new Centenario Stadium, thus featured the two sides that had battled for Olympic gold at the 1928 Olympic Games. Uruguay had won that game narrowly, and the outcome was the same this time. 2-1 down at half-time, Uruguay scored three in the second half to send the great majority of the 90,000-strong crowd into raptures. Montevideo celebrated, a public holiday was declared; the World Cup had exploded onto the sporting calendar.

Uruguay score in the final against Argentina played in Montevideo.

1934 Italy

Italy 2 Czechoslovakia 1

Italy overcome skilful Czechs

Uruguay, still resentful about being snubbed by so many countries in 1930, refused to go to Italy four years later. They remain the only reigning champions not to defend their title.

Thirty-two teams took part in the qualifying round including hosts Italy. This represented a huge increase on the inaugural tournament, though half of the sides were soon on their way home after a single game. The finals proper proceeded on a straight knockout basis. The eight teams that made it through to the second round were all European. There was no more than a single goal in each of the quarter-finals, with Germany, Austria, Italy and Czechoslovakia going through to the last four. Hugo Meisl's brilliant Austrian side were strong favourites to beat Italy, but the host nation squeezed through 1-0 to reach the final. Their opponents were Czechoslovakia, who survived a scare against Germany to run out comfortable 3-1 winners in the end. The Czechs were a very skilful outfit.

They also knew each other extremely well, for the players who took the field in the final came from just two clubs, Sparta and Slavia. No other international side reaching a major final has ever come from such a narrow club base.

Czechs the better side

Czechoslovakia were the better side in the Final, but couldn't convert their superiority into goals. With ten minutes to go they had only a slender one-goal advantage. It wasn't enough. Orsi equalised with a viciously swerving shot, and Schiavio hit the winner for Italy in extra time.

In November that year, the Italians came to Highbury to take on an England team built round the all-conquering Arsenal side. Having been denied the opportunity to show what they could do in the official FIFA tournament, the England players were keen to put one over on the Olympic and world champions. It was dubbed an unofficial decider that would prove which side really was the best in the world. It was a bruising encounter, marred by a string of brutal challenges. England raced into a three-goal lead, the Italians replied with two second-half goals, but couldn't find an equaliser. England had won the battle of Highbury.

Italian players lift up their coach Vittorio Pozzo after winning the trophy in Rome.

Italy 4 Hungary 2

Italy make it two in a row

The 1938 tournament took place against the backdrop of conflict. Spain was already embroiled in a civil war, while Germany's annexation of Austria cast a dark shadow over the future. The fact that the World Cup was played in France the practice of alternating between Europe and the Americas having not yet been established didn't help matters.

There was still no British representation. Only 14 teams contested the finals: 11 European sides, together with Cuba, Brazil and the Dutch East Indies. Italy had built on their 1934 success by winning the 1936 Olympic title in Berlin and was still the team to beat. The tournament was again organised on a straight knockout basis, however, and the holders had their share of luck in narrowly beating Norway 2-1 in the first round. The match between Brazil and Poland provided the most drama. Poland fought back from 3-1 down against a strong Brazilian side to level at 4-4 after 90 minutes. Extra time saw the score reach 5-5, and the deadlock was broken for the final time by Brazil's inside-forward Romeo.

Brazil then needed a replay not to mention a lot of violent play to edge out Czechoslovakia by the odd goal in the second round. In the other quarter-final encounters, Italy eased past the host nation 3-1, while Switzerland the surprise victors over Germany in the opening round fell to the talented Hungarians. Sweden had had a bye in the first round as their opponents, Austria, had been subsumed into the Germany side. The Swedes entered the fray with a resounding 8-0 demolition job of Cuba.

Brazil miss their chance

Brazil rested their star striker Leonidas for their semi-final clash against Italy. The man who had netted four times against Poland was sorely missed. The Brazilians squandered chance after chance, and the Italians hit them with two goals to reach their second final. Their opponents were Hungary, who hammered Sweden 5-1 in the other semi. Both sides had enormous flair, but the Italians also had their trademark steely quality and rugged professionalism. After the holders established a 3-1 half-time lead, they shut their opponents out of the game. Hungary's star forward Sarosi did reduce the arrears with a poacher's goal after 70 minutes, but Piola made sure that the cup would be going back to Italy when he finished off a sublime move eight minutes from time.

Alfredo Foni of Italy tries to reach a cross in the Final against Hungary.

Italian captain Giuseppe Meazza (left) shakes hands with the Hungarian captain Gyorgy Sarosi (right) before the Final played in Paris.

1950 Brazil
Uruguay 2 Brazil 1

England's first World Cup

The 1950 tournament in Brazil saw a return to a group system in the opening stages. It also saw England's first appearance in the finals. FIFA had offered the Home Countries two World Cup places for the 1950 tournament, the winners and runners-up of the Home International competition being awarded automatic qualification. Scotland had to be content with the runners-up spot after losing the decider against England by a single goal. Instead of celebrating the fact that it was still enough to take them to Brazil, Scotland fell victim to an attack of hubris. The Scottish FA had declared that the team would only go if they were champions and so passed up their rightful qualifying place.

England lose to USA

England's inaugural campaign will forever be remembered for the ignominious 1-0 defeat at the hands of the USA. The side had already opened with a win albeit an unimpressive one over Chile. With stars such as Billy Wright, Tom Finney, Stanley

England players and officials arrive home after failing to reach the second round of the competition.

Matthews and Wilf Mannion, England would surely cruise past the USA and justify their position as one of the tournament favourites. England certainly dominated; they were camped in the USA's half for long periods and carved out a host of chances. None was converted, however, and then the unthinkable happened: in the 37th minute Gaetjens deflected a cross past Bert Williams in the England goal. The Americans then held out for the remainder of the match to record a famous victory. A shell-shocked England also lost their final group game, against Spain, and were on their way home.

Late withdrawals

There had been several late withdrawals from the tournament, and only 13 teams had arrived in Brazil to compete for what was now the Jules Rimet Trophy. Spain went forward from England's group with a 100 percent record. Holders Italy surprisingly missed out, unable to recover from their 3-2 defeat by Sweden. Brazil made it through from their group, despite being held to a 2-2 draw by Switzerland. Group Four presented a farcical spectacle: it contained only Uruguay and Bolivia and consisted of a single match which Uruguay won 8-0.

The four teams went through to a second league and another round-robin series. Fortunately for the organisers who had overlooked the fact that there would be no showpiece final - the very last game proved to be the decider. Brazil were a point ahead of Uruguay and needed only a draw for overall victory. 200,000 people poured into Rio's new Maracana Stadium, most anticipating that Brazil were about to be crowned world champions. The first half ended goalless, though the Brazilians were mounting such fluent, incisive attacks that it seemed just a matter of time before the goals went in. One did, just after the break, but Brazil failed to capitalize. Uruguay equalized in the 66th minute through Schiaffino. Brazil still had the cup within their grasp, but they fell away badly and conceded the second killer goal just over ten minutes from time. The planned celebrations to acclaim Brazil's victory were all for nought. Uruguay lifted the trophy for the second time, and as they had not competed in 1934 and 1938, the South Americans thus maintained their 100 per cent record in the competition.

1954 Switzerland
West Germany 3 Hungary 2

Germany beat mighty Magyars

If England had regarded their exit from the 1950 World Cup as a freak occurrence, they soon had no alternative but to accept that there were teams around who had overtaken them in footballing virtuosity. November 1953 has gone down in the annals of the sport as the day when Hungary came to Wembley and gave England a footballing lesson. England had a proud, unblemished home record until the day that Pushkas and Co. came to London and played the game on a totally different level. The visitors won 6-3 at a canter. Six months later, England took a much changed team to Budapest but the result was even more emphatic: a 7-1 drubbing. The Hungarians, who had also taken the 1952 Olympic title, predictably went into the 1954 World Cup in Switzerland as red-hot favourites.

Hungary hit seventeen
The format for the tournament was altered yet again, streamlined into a system which would serve as the template for the next four competitions. The 16 teams to reach the final stages would be split into four groups of four. The top two teams to emerge from the round-robin matches would go forward to the quarter-finals of the tournament, which would then become a knockout competition.

Hungary reinforced their favouritism by hitting 17 goals in their group matches. These goals came from just two matches, for the organisers had decided to seed two teams in each group, with the seeded teams avoiding each other at this stage. West Germany, eventual finalists, were the other team to come through from this group, beating Turkey in a play-off.

Scotland beaten 7-0
The home nations were represented by both England and Scotland. A draw against Belgium and a win over Switzerland saw England through. Scotland lost to a single goal from Austria, and were on the receiving end of a 7-0 beating at the hands of Uruguay. The South American side went on to beat England 4-2 in the quarter-finals. They were joined in the semis by Germany, Hungary, and Austria, the latter having won an extraordinary 7-5 match against Switzerland.

Hungary had got through at the expense of Brazil. What should have been an exhibition of sublime skill descended into a nasty affair: three players were ordered off.

Austria's bubble burst in their semi-final against West Germany, who ran out 6-1 winners. The other semi saw the unbeaten Uruguay take on the brilliant Magyars. Something had to give. Both teams were brilliant but Kocsis scored twice for Hungary in extra-time to clinch a place in the Final.

Pushkas injury
Hungary had beaten West Germany 8-3 in the opening phase, and it looked like being a repeat performance when they went 2-0 up early in the game. The chink in their mighty armour was the great Pushkas, who had been injured in that opening match and not played since. It was the era before substitutes, and Pushkas's insistence on taking the field when he was clearly unfit cost his side dear. The Germans hit back with two goals, then rode their luck as the Hungarians rained efforts on their goal. Seven minutes from time Rahn struck to put Germany 3-2 ahead. The Hungarians did everything but score. The wonder team of the early 1950s couldn't crown their supremacy with a World Cup triumph. That honour went to West Germany, who were a competent, rugged outfit, but nowhere near as good as side as the mighty Magyars.

Max Morlock of West Germany scores his country's first goal in the Final against Hungary.

1958 Sweden

Brazil 5 Sweden 2

Brazil's 17-year-old sensation

The 1958 World Cup took place in Sweden; it was to be the last time that successive tournaments would be staged in the same continent. More significantly as far as the burgeoning media interest in the tournament was concerned, it was the first World Cup to be televised.

All four home nations made it through to the finals, with mixed fortunes. A draw against Yugoslavia was all Scotland had to show for their efforts and they finished as wooden spoonists in their group. England were unbeaten, drawing all three games against the Soviet Union, Brazil and Austria. That was enough for a play-off place, where they went down 1-0 to the Soviet Union. Things might have been different had they not been deprived of the talents of the Manchester United stars killed in the Munich air crash in February of that year. The loss of players of the stature of Duncan Edwards and Tommy Taylor obviously weakened the England side considerably.

Northern Ireland and Wales also made it through to the play-offs. The former beat Czechoslovakia, only to go down 4-0 to France at the quarter-final stage.

Wales defeat Hungarians

Wales did even better. They beat Hungary 2-1, a fine achievement, despite the fact that the Hungarians were not the force they had been four years earlier. In the quarter-finals they faced mighty Brazil, who were emerging as the star team. Wales were hampered by the fact that their inspirational centre-forward John Charles was sidelined through injury. Even so, the Welsh performed heroically and went down by a single goal. It was scored by Brazil's 17-year-old sensation, Pele. The youngest player ever to grace the World Cup finals, Pele was drafted into the side for Brazil's final group game, a 2-0 win over the Soviet Union. The precociously talented youngster had everything: power, pace, balance and mesmerising skills. He also had wonderful vision; he could play team-mates in with a killer pass, yet was a deadly finisher himself, both with his lethal shooting and brilliant heading ability.

Blistering Pele

In the semi-final Brazil were matched against France, who were proving to be a strong and a very attacking side. In four games they had scored 15 goals, with Juste Fontaine becoming something of a goal machine. He was on target against Brazil, too, though it was to be Pele's day. With Brazil only 2-1 ahead at the break, the young star hit a blistering 23-minute hat-trick to put his side out of sight. Their opponents in the Final were the host nation, who had topped Wales' group, then eliminated the Soviet Union and holders West Germany in the knockout stages. Sweden took the lead just four minutes into the game but, unlike 1954, the best team was not to be denied. Brazil hit five yet again, while Sweden managed one second-half consolation goal, by which time the result was not in doubt.

Pele shakes hands with the King of Sweden before the Final.

Pele (right) of Brazil and Kalle Svensson (left) of Sweden compete for the ball during the Final played in Stockholm.

1962 Chile

Brazil 3 Czechoslovakia 1

Brazil lift trophy for second time

Chile 1962 saw Brazil match Italy's feat of the 1930s by recording back-to-back World Cup triumphs. Pele, now a 21-year-old veteran, limped out of the tournament at the group stage. But if the other countries including England thought that Brazil's misfortune improved their own chances, they were soon to be disabused of that notion. Garrincha was in breathtaking form, while Amarildo, the player drafted into the side after Pele was sidelined, proved to be the latest in Brazil's production line of star performers.

The holders' only hiccup on the road to the knockout stage came when they were held to a goalless draw by Czechoslovakia. The Czechs were to be the surprise package of the tournament. Not particularly fancied before the competition started, the Czechs went all the way to the final, where they would meet Brazil for a second time.

England through the first round

England, the only representative from the home countries, sneaked through to the second phase after a mixed bag of performances in their group. They went down 2-1 to Hungary in their opener, performed creditably in a 3-1 win over Argentina, then played out a lacklustre goalless draw against Bulgaria. Second place behind Hungary in the group meant that England had to face Brazil in the quarter-final. Garrincha ran the show, scoring two and making the other in a 3-1 win.

Chile, who had been involved in a violent group match against Italy, surprised many by making it through to the knockout stage. In the last eight they faced the Soviet Union,

The winning Brazil team pictured before the Final played in Santiago.

who boasted the world's best goalkeeper in their side: the great Lev Yashin. It wasn't Yashin's day when he came up against the host nation, however. He let in two shots that he ought to have dealt with comfortably, and a jubilant Chile were through to the semis to face their illustrious South American neighbours, Brazil.

The Chileans quickly found that the tournament favourites were not about to be as charitable as the Soviet Union had been. The gulf in class was all too obvious as Garrincha and Vava grabbed two each in a 4-2 win. The only mishap for Brazil was the fact that Garrincha was sent off for retaliation, something which could have cost him at place in the final. The authorities decided to take a lenient view, noting the extreme provocation that had caused the Brazilian star to react.

Czechoslovakia had beaten Hungary and Yugoslavia in the quarters and semis respectively to earn another crack at Brazil in the showpiece final. The Czechs had certainly performed well above themselves in getting so far, particularly their keeper, Wilhelm Schroiff, who had looked unbeatable. In the five games thus far they had conceded just four goals. On the other hand, they had found the net just six times, so they were hardly a free-scoring side, either.

The world's best team

The Czechs needed to score first, and they did, Masopust firing home in the 16th minute. Against lesser opposition it might have been enough. But Brazil, who had already scored 11 times en route to the final were behind for barely two minutes. Amarildo cut in from the left and hit a glorious shot across Schroiff into the far corner of the net. To their credit, the Czechs held Brazil at bay until 20 minutes from time, when Zito headed home an Amarildo cross. Schroiff then failed to deal with a lob from Santos and Vava pounced on the loose ball to make it 3-1. Brazil lifted the trophy, having enhanced their status as the best team in the world.

Amarildo of Brazil is congratulated by his management team after scoring two goals in the match against Spain.

1966 England

England 4 West Germany 2

Alf Ramsey's victorious England

England's indifferent performance in Chile precipitated a change at the helm. Walter Winterbottom was replaced by Alf Ramsey, the man who had steered Ipswich Town to the 1961-62 League championship in what was the club's first season in the top flight. Ramsey was given a more autonomous role than his predecessor. The FA realised that a supremo taking charge of all England matters was needed if the international side was to make a greater impression on the world stage. The timing was apposite, for England were named as hosts for the next tournament, in 1966.

After a string of impressive results, Ramsey took his side to Brazil in May 1964 for an acid test. The world champions, inspired by Pele, routed England 5-1, and Argentina also beat Ramsey's team. It looked as if it was back to square one for the England boss, and the World Cup was just two years away. As the tournament loomed ever closer, the optimism over England's chances became more muted.

Jules Rimet trophy stolen

In March 1966, just three months before the competition got under way, there was great off-field drama when the Jules

30th July: England on their lap of honour with the trophy (left to right) Banks, Wilson, Ball, Charlton, Moore and Cohen.

Rimet trophy was stolen. The 12-inch-high trophy had been on display in a hall in Westminster. The perpetrator of the crime was never found, but the trophy was recovered in time for the tournament with a little help from a dog called Pickles. The mongrel unearthed it in Norwood, south London. There was a handsome reward for the dog's owner, and the trophy was ready to be fought for by the 16 qualifying teams.

England's progress from the group stage was steady, if unspectacular: a goalless draw against Uruguay, followed by 2-0 wins over both Mexico and France. More interesting was the system adopted. Ramsey decided on a 4-3-3 formation, which meant there was no room for wingers. It was a revolutionary idea at the time, and one which didn't meet with universal support.

The drama of the opening phase centred on the other groups. Incredibly, Brazil failed to qualify, after losing both to Portugal and Hungary. Pele came in for some rough treatment in the two games he played, and returned home threatening not to play in the next tournament.

Italy defeated by North Korea

Italy were another top side to suffer early elimination. After a 2-0 win over Chile, they went down to the Soviet Union by a solitary goal. Needing a result against the minnows of North Korea, the Italians suffered another 1-0 defeat and were on the plane home, where they were subjected to liberal helpings of abuse and rotten fruit.

Argentina and an impressive German side had emerged from Group 2, and the former were England's quarter-final opponents. It was an ill-tempered game, with Argentina's captain Antonio Rattin among the chief culprits. Eventually, the West German referee had had enough and ordered Rattin off. Initially, he refused to go, and there was chaos for several minutes before he finally left the field. England won the game with a header from Geoff Hurst, the West Ham striker who had only broken into the England team a few months earlier.

Eusebio rescues Portugal

Portugal and the great Eusebio were England's semi-final opponents. The Portuguese had cantered through their three group matches, scoring nine goals in the process. They then had the scare of their lives when North Korea, conquerors of Italy, went three up in the first half of their quarter-final encounter at Goodison Park. Enter Eusebio, who hit back with four goals of his own to help his side to a 5-3 win.

Eusebio scored his ninth goal of the tournament in the semi-final against England, but it wasn't enough; two rasping strikes from Bobby Charlton won the game for England. Eusebio

The winning England team pose with the Jules Rimet trophy. Top row (left to right) trainer Harold Shepperdson, Nobby Stiles, Roger Hunt, Gordon Banks, Jack Charlton, George Cohen, Ray Wilson and manager Alf Ramsey. Bottom row: Martin Peters, Geoff Hurst, Bobby Moore, Alan Ball and Bobby Charlton.

would have the consolation of finishing the tournament as top scorer.

The Germans had made impressive progress throughout the tournament. There were victories over Switzerland and Spain in the first round, together with a draw against the temperamental and cynical Argentinians. They thumped Uruguay 4-0 in the quarter-final and edged out the Soviet Union by the odd goal in the semis.

It was Germany who struck first in the final, their top scorer Helmut Haller slotting home after 12 minutes. Six minutes later, Hurst headed home a Bobby Moore free kick to equalise. Martin Peters, the third of the West Ham contingent in the side, hit what looked to be the winner in the second half, pouncing on a poor clearance from the German defence. With seconds to go, Wolfgang Weber scrambled the ball into the net from a free kick and the match went into extra time.

Hurst the hat-trick hero

In the first period, Hurst scored what remains the most controversial goal in footballing history. He controlled an Alan Ball cross, swivelled and thudded his shot against the underside of the bar. There was an agonising wait as the referee consulted his Russian linesman. The latter nodded emphatically, indicating that the ball had crossed the line.

In the dying seconds, Hurst latched onto a long clearance from Moore, raced clear and hammered the ball past a statuesque Tilkowski into the roof of the net. For Hurst it was a personal triumph; he remains the only player ever to score a hat-trick in a World Cup final. For Ramsey it was the realization of a long-held dream. He had set his sights on World Cup victory as soon as he was appointed. England had now joined an elite group consisting of just five countries who had won international football's ultimate prize.

Below and opposite: England's controversial third goal (Hurst's second). The ball bounces out of the goal as the German goalkeeper, Hans Tilkowski, is beaten.

1966 Results

GROUP 1

	P	W	D	L	F	A	Pts
England	3	2	1	0	4	0	5
Uruguay	3	1	2	0	2	1	4
Mexico	3	0	2	1	1	3	2
France	3	0	1	2	2	5	1

England	0	Uruguay	0
France	1	Mexico	1
Uruguay	2	France	1
England	2	Mexico	0
Uruguay	0	Mexico	0
England	2	France	0

GROUP 2

	P	W	D	L	F	A	Pts
W.Germany	3	2	1	0	8	2	5
Argentina	3	1	1	1	4	3	3
Spain	3	1	1	1	2	3	3
Switzerland	3	0	1	2	1	7	1

W.Germany	5	Switzerland	0
Argentina	2	Spain	1
Spain	2	Switzerland	1
Argentina	2	Switzerland	0
W.Germany	2	Spain	1
W.Germany	2	Spain	1

GROUP 3

	P	W	D	L	F	A	Pts
Portugal	3	3	0	0	9	2	6
Hungary	3	2	0	1	7	5	4
Brazil	3	1	0	2	4	6	2
Bulgaria	3	0	0	3	1	8	0

Brazil	2	Bulgaria	0
Portugal	3	Hungary	1
Hungary	3	Brazil	1
Portugal	3	Bulgaria	0
Portugal	3	Brazil	1
Hungary	3	Bulgaria	1

GROUP 4

	P	W	D	L	F	A	Pts
Sov.Union	3	3	0	0	6	1	6
N.Korea	3	1	1	1	2	4	3
Italy	3	1	0	2	2	2	2
Chile	3	0	1	2	2	5	1

Sov.Union	3	N.Korea	0
Italy	2	Chile	0
Chile	1	N.Korea	1
Sov.Union	1	Italy	0
N.Korea	1	Italy	0
Sov.Union	2	Chile	1

QUARTER-FINALS

England	1	Argentina	0
W.Germany	4	Uruguay	0
Portugal	5	N.Korea	3
Sov. Union	2	Hungary	1

SEMI-FINALS

W. Germany 2 (Haller 44, Beckenbauer 68)
Sov. Union 1 (Porkuyan 88)

England 2 (R Charlton 30, 79)
Portugal 1 (Eusebio 82)

3rd PLACE PLAY-OFF Portugal 2 (Eusebio 12, Torres 88)
Sov. Union 1 (Metreveli 43)

FINAL   July 30 – Wembley Stadium

England   **4**   (Hurst 19, 100, 119, Peters 77)
W. Germany **2**   (Haller 13, Weber 89)

AET HT: 1-1 90min 2-2.   Att: 96,924.   Ref: Dienst (Swi)

England   Banks, Cohen, Wilson, Stiles, J Charlton, Moore,
                 Ball, Hunt, R Charlton, Hurst, Peters

West Germany   Tilkowski, Höttges, Schnellinger, Beckenbauer, Schülz,
                 Weber, Haller, Overath, Seeler, Held, Emmerich.

TOP SCORER   Eusebio (Por) 9 goals

1970 Mexico

Brazil 4 Italy 1

Brazil claim Jules Rimet trophy for third win

England were once again Britain's sole representative in the 1970 World Cup, held in Mexico. This time, of course, the stakes were higher as Ramsay's men were defending champions. Many of the heroes of '66 were still there: Banks, Charlton, Moore and Peters. The newer breed included Terry Cooper and Brian Labone in defence, Alan Mullery and Colin Bell in midfield, and Francis Lee and Jeff Astle up front. Most pundits thought it a stronger squad than the one that had lifted the trophy four years earlier.

One big difference between 1966 and 1970 was the climate. England not only had to contend with opponents such as a resurgent Brazilian side and Italy, winners of the 1968 European Nations Cup; the players also had to deal with the searing heat and enervating humidity of the Mexican summer. England were drawn in Brazil's group. Like England, Brazil had a blend of the old and the new. Pele, now in his fourth World Cup, was at the height of his powers. Then there was Rivelino, noted for his thunderous shots from distance; Gerson, a brilliant midfield general; and Jairzinho, a prodigiously talented wide player who was also deadly in front of goal.

Gordon Bank's sensational save

The England Brazil clash was settled when Pele set up Jairzinho to crash home the only goal of the game in the second half. Earlier, the roles had been reversed as Jairzinho skipped past Cooper and crossed perfectly for Pele, whose powerful downward header was going just inside the post. Banks threw himself to his right and somehow scooped the ball over the bar. It was hailed as one of the greatest saves of any World Cup tournament.

Gordon Banks makes a remarkable save from a header by Pele during their first round match.

England had their share of chances in the game but failed to convert any of them. There were hugs and smiles all round at the end, and many believed that these two quality sides might well meet again at the knockout stage.

Both teams enjoyed victories over Czechoslovakia and Romania and progressed to the quarter-finals. Brazil took on Peru and eased into the semis with a 4-2 win, Jairzinho keeping up his record of scoring in every game. England, by contrast, let a two-goal lead slip against their old adversaries West Germany. Ramsey's team seemed to be cruising into the last four, thanks to goals from Mullery and Peters. The imperious Beckenbauer then drove a shot past Bonnetti, who was playing because Banks had a stomach upset. A back header from the diminutive Seeler looped agonisingly over Bonnetti's head to force extra time. England's misery was complete when Gerd Muller "Der Bomber" volleyed home from close range and sealed a 3-2 win.

Brazil's sparkling display

Brazil cruised through their semi against Uruguay, while the other match, Germany v Italy, provided the tournament's most dramatic encounter. Italy took an early lead, then relied on their customary mean defence to see them through. Germany equalised with seconds to go to take the game into extra time. Five goals flew in during that 30-minute period. Rivera had the last word in the goal-fest and clinched a place in the final for Italy.

The final was a classic showdown between the exuberant flair of the Brazilians and the

dour, methodical approach adopted by the Italians. The former triumphed in what was a sparkling display of incisive and inventive football. Pele scored one and laid on two in a 4-1 win. Brazil, as three-time winners of the tournament, claimed the Jules Rimet trophy outright.

Brazilian legend Pele training.

1974 West Germany
West Germany 2 Holland 1

Dutch masters beaten by West Germany

Notwithstanding England's World Cup win in 1966, Brazil remained the team of the decade. By 1974, the balance of world footballing power had shifted. Not to the winners of the competition, either. That honour went to the host nation, West Germany. The Germans had won 1972 European Nations Cup in fine style, and boasted players of stature are of Gerd Muller, Paul Breitner and "The Kaiser" himself, Franz Beckenbauer. But the team of the tournament was undoubtedly Holland, led by the man who had taken over Pele's mantle as the world's best player, Johann Cruyff.

Total Football

The Dutch were the architects of Total Football. They disdainfully tossed aside all the tactical arguments about formations and systems and went out and played a fluid style which was both innovative and exhilarating. The players were not labelled by their positions; defenders, who were also marvellous ball players, would drift into the attack, forwards would drop deep to cover. It was a style which had made Ajax the top club side in Europe, bringing them the European Cup three years in succession. Now, Total Football was about to be unleashed on the world.

Unsurprisingly, Holland topped their group, although they were held to a draw by Sweden. West and East Germany emerged comfortably from their group. Scotland flew the flag for the home countries but were edged out of a quarter-final place on goal difference by Yugoslavia and Brazil, all three teams finishing on four points.

England had failed to qualify, thanks to that fateful Wembley night in October 1973, when the team threw

Johann Cruyff of Holland jumps a tackle from Uli Hoeness of West Germany during the final.

everything at Poland but were held to a 1-1 draw. Ramsey was sacked from the England job for failing to qualify ahead of Poland and Wales. But Poland were to be the revelation of the tournament. They scored 12 goals on their way to topping their group with maximum points, beating Italy and Argentina along the way. Poland's form meant that Italy, finalists in 1970, were relegated to third place in the group and were out.

The eight teams to emerge from the first phase were put into two new groups, a change from the straight knockout system of the previous five competitions. Poland and West Germany both beat Sweden and Yugoslavia and faced each other in the final game, effectively a sudden death semi-final. Germany won 1-0 and went through to the final. Poland finished the competition a worthy third, small consolation for England fans.

Holland's penalty drama

Holland also had a 100 percent record in the second phase. Most commentators believed - and all neutrals hoped - that the Dutch would go on to be crowned world champions. When they went one up just seconds into the Final, all expectations looked about to be realized. Johann Cruyff, with his customary beautiful balance and superb control, jinked his way into the opposition's box, where he was brought down by a despairing tackle from Uli Hoeness. Britain's top referee Jack Taylor had no hesitation in awarding a penalty. Neeskens scored from the spot; it was the fastest goal ever scored in a World Cup final.

West Germany were second best for a long period, but they were resilient and dangerous. The Dutch failed to convert their superiority into further goals and paid the price. West Germany equalised with a penalty of their own. Then, two

minutes from half-time, the great Gerd Muller spun and drilled the ball low into the corner of the net. The game ended 2-1, the Dutch masters having to settle for the runners-up spot, while the victorious Germans joined the exclusive club of two-time World Cup winners.

*Muller (left) and Breitner
celebrate West Germany s victory.*

*Gerd Muller (right) of West Germany holds the trophy aloft as his team-
mate Overath waves to the crowd.*

1978 Argentina
Argentina 3 Holland 1

Ally's Army miss out

There was disappointment once again in the England ranks as the team failed to reach the 1978 finals in Argentina. The team's inability to run up enough goals against Luxembourg and Finland was the problem. Italy, the other big name in their qualifying group, piled up the goals against the minnows and went to the party instead of England on goal difference. Don Revie, the man who had taken over after Ramsey's departure, saw the writing on the wall and quit even before the qualifying series was over. Ron Greenwood inherited an impossible situation, and England fans were confined to a spectator's role as the carnival in Argentina got under way.

Scotland were there again, though. The Scots had dashed Wales' hopes of qualifying in a controversial game at Anfield. A hotly-disputed handball decision turned the game. Don Masson scored from the spot and Kenny Dalglish rubbed salt into the Welsh wounds in the dying minutes. It was a bitter pill for Mike Smith's team to swallow. They stayed at home while Ally MacLeod's Scotland, along with "Ally's Army" of fans prepared for the long haul to South America.

Johann Cruyff had declined to make the trip for Holland, but the Dutch had many of their stars from 1974, and football purists everywhere had Holland as their second favourite team.

Gemmill's solo effort

Holland and Scotland found themselves in the same group. The Scots, boasting an array of talent including Dalglish, Jordan, Buchan and Gemmill went into the tournament with high hopes. They notched a famous of 3-2 victory over Neeskens, Rep and Co., in the final round-robin game, but it wasn't enough. MacLeod's men had gone down 3-1 to Peru and could only draw 1-1 with Iran. For the second tournament running, the Scots missed out on goal average. They at least had the consolation of scoring the tournament's best goal: a sensational solo effort from Archie Gemmill in the win over Holland.

Italy and Argentina had both beaten Hungary and France when they met in Group One. Italy scored the only goal of the game, but both teams were comfortably through.

Gonella, the Italian referee, looks at his watch as an Argentinian player lies on the ground during the Final against Holland.

Poland showed that 1974 was no fluke by topping Group Two. West Germany squeezed through with them. The Germans finished a point ahead of Tunisia, with whom they could only draw in their final group match.

An unimpressive Brazil side drew with Sweden and Spain and went through after a narrow 1-0 win over Austria, who topped the group.

Argentina win on home soil

Holland stepped up a gear in the second phase. After wins over Austria and Italy, a 2-2 draw with West Germany saw them into the final again. Brazil and Argentina drew 0-0 and both beat Poland and Peru. It all came down to goal difference, and Argentina came out on top, thanks to the six goals they had put past Peru in the final game.

Mario Kempes, the tournament's top striker, gave Argentina a 1-0 lead at half-time. They held the advantage until nine minutes from time, when Nanninga headed an equaliser. Two goals in extra time settled the match. Kempes scored with a brilliant individual effort, then set up Bertoni for the goal which sealed victory.

A passionate 80,000-strong crowd at the River Plate stadium gave their team an amazing ticker-tape reception. Argentina had boycotted the 1938, 1950 and 1954 tournaments; the 1966 side had been branded "animals" by Ramsey; now Argentina had finally taken their place at the top table of international football, becoming only the sixth country to lift the World Cup.

Kenny Dalglish, Scotland's star striker

Colleco of Argentina fouls Dalglish of Scotland in a world cup warm up match in Beunos Aires.

1982 Spain
Italy 3 West Germany 1

Italy's third success

After missing two World Cups, England made it to Spain 1982, albeit after a very scratchy qualifying series. A first-ever defeat against Norway, a team made up of mostly part-timers, left them needing results involving Romania, Switzerland and Hungary to go their way. Fortune was on the side of Ron Greenwood's men, and England secured qualification with a 1-0 win over Hungary in their final qualifying match.

Scotland and Northern Ireland both made it through from the same group, giving the home countries their greatest degree of representation in the finals since 1958. All three took their place in an extended 24-team tournament. One famous name missing from the list was Holland. The team of the 1970s failed at the first hurdle in 1982.

England off to a flying start

In the first of their group games, against France, England captain Bryan Robson scored with a header after just 27 seconds. Further victories over Czechoslovakia and Kuwait saw Greenwood's men through to the second phase with a 100 per cent record. More unlikely group winners were Northern Ireland, who drew against Yugoslavia and Honduras, then scored a famous 1-0 win over hosts Spain. Scotland were unlucky yet again, going out on goal difference for the third tournament running.

Northern Ireland drew with Austria but were thumped 4-1 by France in the second phase. They went home with heads held high, and in 17-year-old Norman Whiteside they boasted the youngest ever player to grace the finals.

England's interest ended at the same stage after their matches against West Germany and Spain both ended in goalless draws. Spain only had pride to play for when they faced England. England needed to win by two goals to progress at the expense of West Germany. Hampered by the fact that

Paulo Rossi of Italy is pusued by Paul Breitner of West Germany during the Italian 3–1 victory in the Final.

Brooking and Keegan were only fit enough to play half an hour, England didn't have the creativity or fire power to make it to the semis.

German's beat classy French

The Germans went on to meet France in the last four. The French midfield trio of Michel Platini, Alain Giresse and Jean Tigana were at the heart of a classy outfit. They went into a 3-1 lead, but conceded two late goals to provide the World Cup with its first penalty shoot-out. Neutrals sided with the French. Not only was their play more stylish, but in the opening phase the Germans had been party to one of the most disgraceful matches ever seen in the competition. They played out a cynical 1-0 win in their final group match against Austria. This scoreline suited both countries, who knew that they would both go through at the expense of Algeria, the latter having already completed their fixtures.

The Germans lost even more friends during the semi-final, when their 'keeper Harald Schumacher knocked out French striker Patrick Battiston with a sickening flying tackle. The neutrals didn't get their way, though: West Germany won 5-4 on penalties.

Italy and Poland, who had emerged from the same group, contested the other semi-final. Poland had topped the table, while Italy had drawn all three games and narrowly edged out Cameroon on goal difference. The Italians improved as the competition went on, however. In the second phase they beat holders Argentina and favourites Brazil. The Italy Brazil game was the tournament's best. A thrilling game of fluctuating fortunes saw Paolo Rossi put Italy ahead three times. Brazil came back twice but a third equaliser eluded them.

Rossi then grabbed both goals in a 2-0 win over Poland in the semis. The Poles went on to finish third, as they had in 1974, while Italy marched on to face West Germany in the final.

Rossi the Italian hotshot

The showpiece was no classic, but the result was the right one. The Italians shrugged off a penalty miss to score three second-half goals. Rossi got the first of them and confirmed himself as the tournament's hotshot with six goals. He then laid on the second for Tardelli, and Altobelli added a third ten minutes from time. Germany scored a late consolation goal but it was Enzo Bearzot's Italy who joined Brazil as the only teams to win the World Cup on three occasions.

Socrates of Brazil moves in between Graeme Souness (left) and David Narey (right) of Scotland during their match in Seville.

Serginho of Brazil takes on Ramon Diaz (right) of Argentina during their second round game.

1986 Mexico

Argentina 3 West Germany 2

Maradona's 'Hand of God'

England headed for Mexico in the summer 1986 after finishing top of their qualifying group, unbeaten. Bobby Robson, the man who had steered Ipswich Town to the top of the domestic game, and won both the FA and UEFA cups, was now in charge. Northern Ireland, who were in England's group, were also able to pack their bags, thanks to a hard-fought goalless draw at Wembley. Scotland made it, too, after a dramatic and controversial match against Wales. The Welsh needed to win and held a 1-0 advantage, when a controversial penalty was awarded. Davie Cooper scored from the spot and the Scots went through via the play-offs. The match was overshadowed by the death of Scotland boss Jock Stein, who collapsed in the tunnel at Ninian Park seconds before the final whistle.

England went some way to exorcising the ghost of not 1973 by beating Poland 3-0 - a Gary Lineker hat-trick - to secure second place in the group. It was a welcome scoreline, following a 1-0 defeat by Portugal and a goalless draw with Morocco, the eventual group winners. Third-placed Poland still progressed, however, thanks to a farcical piece of organisation from FIFA. Not only did the top two teams from the six groups go through, but the four best third-placed teams joined them in the second phase. Thus, the 36 group games merely whittled the 24 teams down to 16.

Scotland and Northern Ireland miss out

Northern Ireland were one of the third-placed sides to miss out, with only a draw against Algeria to show for their efforts. They were beaten by the two powerhouse sides in their group, Brazil and Spain.

Scotland were also on the plane home after notching a solitary point against Uruguay. They were unlucky, Group E being dubbed the "Group of Death". The Scots lost by the odd goal to both West Germany and Denmark, the latter, along with Brazil, having the only hundred percent records during the group stage.

From now on the tournament was knock-out all the way. England eased into the quarter-finals with a 3-0 win over Paraguay. Lineker grabbed two more, with Peter Beardsley also on target. France beat Italy 2-0 to set up a clash with Brazil, who were comfortable 4-0 winners over Poland. West Germany squeezed past Morocco 1-0, with coach Franz Beckenbauer playing down his side's chances. The two best games saw Spain do a 5-1 demolition job on the previously unbeaten Danes, while the impressive Belgians put out the Soviet Union in a seven-goal thriller. These two sides would now face each other.

Maradona seals Argentinian victory

England's quarter-final opponents were Argentina, who boasted the world's greatest player, Diego Maradona. The diminutive genius showed his best

'Hand of God' - Maradona slaps the ball past Peter Shilton

and worst sides during the match. In the 51st minute he rose to challenge Peter Shilton for a high ball in the area. With no chance of making contact with his head, Maradona slapped the ball past the England 'keeper into the net. While replays clearly showed the offence, neither referee nor linesman spotted the goal which Maradona later claimed had been partly down to the "hand of God".

Four minutes later, with England still reeling from the decision, Maradona danced his way through half the England side before slotting the ball past Shilton to score one of the best ever World Cup goals. Lineker got one back for England to put him on six goals for the tournament, but it was Argentina who marched on.

Maradona's men finally halted Belgium's progress in the semis. The 2-0 scoreline was matched by West Germany, who ended France's hopes of adding the world crown to the European championship they had won in 1984.

Argentina took a two-goal lead in the Final, but the Germans showed their famous World Cup pedigree by drawing level with goals from Rummenigge and Voller, the equaliser coming 8 minutes from time. Fittingly, Maradona made the decisive goal, setting up Burruchaga to slot home the winner. He confirmed that he was the world's top player during the tournament, yet had been guilty of one of the most blatant pieces of cheating ever seen on a football field.

Gary Lineker in action against Paraguay. England went on to win 3-0.

Maradona takes on Sansom and Butcher of England

1990 Italy
West Germany 1 Argentina 0

England's penalty agony

Jack Charlton, one of England's 1966 heroes, led the Republic of Ireland to their first appearance in the World Cup finals in 1990. England and Scotland both made it through to Italia '90, too, giving the British Isles three representatives in the finals for the third time running.

The draw pitted England and the Republic against each other in the opening phase, along with Ruud Gullit's Holland, the reigning champions of Europe. FIFA persisted with the same format as 1986, and all three teams progressed to the knockout stage. England started slowly, drawing against the Republic and Holland, then scraping a 1-0 win over eventual wooden spoonists Egypt. It was enough to take Bobby Robson's men through as group winners, as both the Republic and Holland drew all three games.

Only Italy and Brazil emerged from the group stage with three wins under their belt. Scotland were in the latter's group, and although they only went down 1-0 to the three-time winners, they had lost 1-0 to the minnows of Costa Rica. A solid 2-1 win over Sweden meant that the Scots finished in third place in the group on two points. Unfortunately, four other third-placed teams had done better, and Scotland maintained their unenviable record of failing to progress beyond the group stage in six attempts.

Cameroon sparkle

Champions Argentina fared little better, scraping through in third place in their group, behind Cameroon and Romania. Cameroon, who were a breath of fresh air, had got the competition off to the most dramatic start by beating the holders 1-0. Maradona was still there, and inspirational in flashes, but Argentina won few friends as they progressed through the tournament.

The holders were very lucky to knock arch rivals Brazil out 1-0 in the second round. England got past Belgium by the

Diego Maradona of Argentina argues with the referee during the match against Germany.

same score. The Belgians had impressed in 1986 and were again a formidable proposition. In the dying seconds of extra-time, Paul Gascoigne, one of the players of the tournament, floated a free kick into Belgium's box. David Platt met it with the sweetest of volleys and planted it into the net.

Republic of Ireland in the last eight

The Republic's dream continued, too, as Jack Charlton's men also made it to the last eight by beating Romania on penalties, after a goalless game. There they came up against the host nation, 2-0 winners over Uruguay in the last 16. Ireland went out to a single goal from Salvator "Toto" Schillaci - who went on to be the competition's top scorer having made many friends along the way.

Argentina were again unimpressive in their win over Yugoslavia on penalties. West Germany made it through to the semis for an incredible ninth time in 12 attempts. A 1-0 win over Czechoslovakia set up a mouth-watering clash with England in the last four. England had finally ended the Cameroon jamboree in the quarter-finals, though not without a scare. Platt put England ahead, but Cameroon hit back with two second-half goals. In the end, the African team's naivety cost them, for they were unable to close the game down. They gave away two reckless penalties and Lineker converted both to take England into a semi-final against the old enemy.

Penalty drama

England went behind to a cruelly-deflected free kick which looped over Shilton. Lineker equalised with a great poacher's strike and the teams were still locked at 1-1 after extra time. Before the drama of a penalty shoot-out, the tournament had one of its most memorable moments when Gascoigne broke down in tears after receiving a booking which would have kept him out of the final. That was academic, however, as Waddle and Pearce both missed from the spot and broke English hearts.

In the other semi, Argentina and Italy were also drawing after extra time and the South American side's luck held for yet another penalty shoot-out. In their six matches, Argentina had won two, drawn three and lost one in open play.

In a poor Final, Argentina seemed to believe their best hope of beating Germany lay in the yet another shoot-out. Two Argentinian players were sent off, and the only goal of the game was scored from the spot by Brehme, after a foul on Voller. Those decisions might have been marginal, but the Argentinians were at their cynical worst and it would have been a travesty had they retained the trophy.

Paul Gascoigne breaks down in tears after receiving a booking which would have kept him out of the final.

Pat Bonner, Republic of Ireland goalkeeper, makes a save in the penalty shoot-out against Romania in the second round.

1994 USA

Brazil 0 Italy 0 (Brazil 3-2 on penalties)

Brazil win penalty shoot-out

The FA's decision to dispense with Bobby Robson's services and draft in Graham Taylor after 1990 soon looked very hollow. After a dire showing in the 1992 European Nations Cup, England failed to qualify for USA '94. The semi-finalists of Italia '90 lost out to Holland and Norway and even went 1-0 behind in less than 10 seconds to San Marino. Although the team recovered to win that game 7-1, it wasn't enough; Taylor's reign was over. Scotland, Wales and Northern Ireland also failed to qualify; it was the first time in the pos-twar era that there would be no United Kingdom representation at the World Cup.

Jack Charlton's men were there again, though. The Republic proved that 1990 was no fluke and made it through to the second round in the tightest group of all. Mexico, Italy and Norway provided the opposition and all four teams won, drew and lost a match. FIFA had introduced three points for a

Jack Charlton celebrates the final whistle as Ireland defeat Italy 1-0.

win, so each team finished on four points. Norway, one of the teams who had made it to the USA at England's expense, was the country to miss out on goal difference.

Nigeria top group

Unlike the Republic, Cameroon came back to earth with a bump. They finished bottom of their group, with just one point from a draw against Sweden, who went through with favourites Brazil. Another African side did make its mark, however. Nigeria were hugely entertaining in their wins over Bulgaria and Greece. They did go down 2-1 to Argentina, but had done enough to top the group.

A seemingly rejuvenated Maradona, now 33, had orchestrated a victory over Greece, as well as Nigeria. But after the latter game he failed a routine drugs test and his tournament was over.

Colombia eliminated

The USA were not just content to host the party. After a draw against Switzerland, they beat Colombia, many people's dark horses to go all the way. Despite a 1-0 defeat against the impressive Romania in the final group match, the USA had done enough to progress as one of the best third-placed sides. Colombia finishing bottom and being eliminated at the first hurdle was one of the big shocks of the competition. It precipitated a tragedy which overshadowed matters on the pitch. Andres Escobar, who had scored an own goal in his country's 2-1 defeat by the USA, was shot dead shortly after returning home.

The Republic came up against a Holland side who had topped their group, but only after unimpressive wins over Saudi Arabia and Morocco. Defensive mistakes gifted the Dutch two goals, though, and Charlton's team was out.

There were no major surprises en route to the quarter-finals. Germany put out Belgium in an entertaining 3-2 match; Spain and Sweden eliminated Switzerland and Saudi Arabia respectively; the USA left the stage with heads held high, going down only 1-0 to Brazil. Italy had a mighty scare against Nigeria; 1-0 down with seconds to go, Roberto Baggio equalised, then scored the winner from the spot in extra time.

One of the most surprising and refreshing aspects of the competition was the form shown by East European sides Romania and Bulgaria. The Bulgarians beat Mexico in the only penalty shoot-out of the second round. Romania, inspired by Hagi, were 3-2 winners over an Argentina side robbed of Maradona's skills.

Germans crash out

Bulgaria went on to send Germany crashing out of the competition in the quarter-finals. They overturned a 1-0 scoreline with two late goals to make it into the semis, having achieved nothing in the five World Cups in which they had competed previously. Romania came within an inch of joining them, but went down on penalties after drawing 2-2 with Sweden. Brazil edged out Holland in a five goal thriller, while Baggio again proved to be Italy's ace with a late winner against Spain.

Baggio was also the man to finally prick Bulgaria's bubble, his two first-half goals enough to see Italy into their fifth World Cup final. Their opponents were Brazil, who beat Sweden more comfortably than the 1-0 scoreline suggested.

Having finished third in their group and had plenty of luck in getting past Nigeria, Spain and Bulgaria, the Italians were negative in the Final. It appeared that they were happy to play for a draw and penalties, and they got their wish. Fortunately for football, Brazil won the shoot-out after Italy's golden boy Baggio blazed over the bar with his spot kick.

Paul McGrath of the Republic of Ireland tackles Holland's Denis Bergkamp.

Dino Baggio brings down Mazinho of Brazil during the Final.

1998 France

Brazil 0 France 3

Zidane the French architect

An expanded 32 team tournament in France '98 meant an end to first round groups where three of the four teams often went through. Now it was the top two from each of the eight groups to go through to the last 16.

After the glories of Euro '96, England were tipped to do well in France. There was a hiccup against Romania when Chelsea's Dan Petrescu scored the winner in a 2-1 victory. But wins over Tunisia and Colombia ensured England's passage.

Liverpool's teenage prodigy Michael Owen had come off the bench to score in the Romania game. He now looked a certainty to start for England in the knockout stage.

Not for the first time, Scotland found themselves in Brazil's group. The two sides met in the curtain raiser, the Scots going down bravely 2-1, their cause not helped by a Tommy Boyd own goal. A draw against a dangerous Norway team followed, but Scotland fell apart in their final match, losing 3-0 to Morocco and once again finishing the bottom of their group. In fact, even had they won the match it wouldn't have been enough, for Norway upset the odds by beating Brazil and joining them in the second phase.

Shocks of the first round included Nigeria and Paraguay going forward at the expense of the dangerous Spain and Bulgaria, the latter having reached the semi-final four years earlier. Meanwhile, France and Argentina were the only sides to emerge from the group stage with an unblemished record.

England players look on in disbelief as David Beckham is sent off after kicking Diego Simeone of Argentina during the second round match.

Owen's wonder goal

England's clash with Argentina proved to be the most dramatic of the second phase. A penalty apiece, both converted, left the sides locked at 1-1. Michael Owen then scored the goal of the tournament, picking the ball up in a deep position and running at the heart of the Argentina defence before rifling his shot into the top corner. Argentina levelled from a clever free kick, and after David Beckham's dismissal for a petulant piece of retaliation on Diego Simeone, the balance looked to have swung the South Americans' way. Ten-man England thought they had scored a Golden Goal in extra time, but Sol Campbell's towering header was ruled out for an innocuous-looking infringement. It went to penalties, where England suffered yet another shoot-out defeat, David Batty the man to miss the vital kick on this occasion.

Brazil and Denmark were the most comfortable Round Two winners; they put out Chile and Nigeria respectively, the scoreline 4-1 in each case. All the other games were won by the odd goal. In France's case it was a Golden Goal: Laurent Blanc scoring to end Paraguay's interest in dramatic fashion.

France again looked short of fire-power in their quarter-final match against Italy. The home nation needed penalties to progress to the last four, and at that stage looked the least impressive of the semi-finalists. Croatia, on the other hand, showed excellent form in dumping the Germans out unceremoniously 3-0. Holland beat Argentina 2-1, their late winner from Bergkamp rivalling Owen's strike as a sublime piece of skill. And the ever-dangerous Brazil, with Ronaldo firing the bullets, came out on top 3-2 after a terrific battle with Denmark.

Michael Owen shrugs off Jose Chamot of Argentina.

Thuram's goal spree

Most people's favourites probably came from the Brazil Holland semi-final. Brazil won it on penalties, after the match ended 1-1. France sent home fans wild by beating Croatia 2-1. Their goalscoring problem on the day was solved by full-back Lillian Thuram, who popped up with the two goals that won the match. Davor Suker provided Croatia's only reply and took the prestigious Golden Boot award.

Rumours over Ronaldo's fitness were quashed when he was named in the side to face France, having initially been left out. The world's premier striker was clearly out of sorts, however, and Brazil as a whole were lacklustre in the Final. France, by contrast, finally began to show their mettle as an attractive, attacking side. Zinedine Zidane, so often the brilliant architect, scored twice with his head, and Petit sealed a comprehensive win when he stroked home a third. Sixty-eight years and 16 tournaments after two Frenchmen saw their dream of a World Cup realized, Les Bleus had finally brought the trophy home.

Right: Ronaldo leaves the field wearing his runners-up medal after loosing the final 3-0 to France.
Below: France's winning team pictured before the Final played in the Stade de France.
Opposite: France's goalkeeper, Barthez, goes head over heels in search of World Cup glory.

1998 Results

GROUP A

	P	W	D	L	F	A	Pts
Brazil	3	2	0	1	6	3	6
Norway	3	1	2	0	5	4	5
Morocco	3	1	1	1	5	5	4
Scotland	3	0	1	2	2	6	1

Brazil	2	Scotland	1
Morocco	2	Norway	2
Brazil	3	Morocco	0
Scotland	1	Norway	1
Brazil	1	Norway	2
Scotland	0	Morocco	3

GROUP B

	P	W	D	L	F	A	Pts
Italy	3	2	1	0	7	2	7
Chile	3	0	3	0	4	4	3
Austria	3	0	2	1	3	4	2
Cameroon	3	0	2	1	2	5	2

Italy	2	Chile	2
Austria	1	Cameroon	1
Chile	1	Austria	1
Italy	3	Cameroon	0
Chile	1	Cameroon	1
Italy	2	Austria	1

GROUP C

	P	W	D	L	F	A	Pts
France	3	3	0	0	9	1	9
Denmark	3	1	1	1	3	3	4
S.Africa	3	0	2	1	3	6	2
S.Arabia	3	0	1	2	2	7	1

S.Arabia	0	Denmark	1
France	3	S.Africa	0
France	4	S.Arabia	0
S.Africa	1	Denmark	1
France	2	Denmark	1
S.Africa	2	S.Arabia	2

GROUP D

	P	W	D	L	F	A	Pts
Nigeria	3	2	0	1	5	5	6
Paraguay	3	1	2	0	3	1	5
Spain	3	1	1	1	8	4	4
Bulgaria	3	0	1	2	1	7	1

Paraguay	0	Bulgaria	0
Spain	2	Nigeria	3
Nigeria	1	Bulgaria	0
Spain	0	Paraguay	0
Nigeria	1	Paraguay	3
Spain	6	Bulgaria	1

GROUP E

	P	W	D	L	F	A	Pts
Holland	3	1	2	0	7	2	5
Mexico	3	1	2	0	7	5	5
Belgium	3	0	3	0	3	3	3
S. Korea	3	0	1	2	2	9	1

S.Korea	1	Mexico	3
Holland	2	Belgium	0
Belgium	2	Mexico	2
Holland	5	S.Korea	0
Belgium	1	S.Korea	1
Holland	2	Mexico	2

GROUP F

	P	W	D	L	F	A	Pts
Germany	3	2	1	0	6	2	7
Yugoslavia	3	2	1	0	4	2	7
Iran	3	1	0	2	2	4	3
USA	3	0	0	3	1	5	0

Germany	2	USA	0
Yugoslavia	1	Iran	0
Germany	2	Yugoslavia	2
USA	1	Iran	2
Germany	2	Iran	0
USA	0	Yugoslavia	1

GROUP G

	P	W	D	L	F	A	Pts
Romania	3	2	1	0	4	2	7
England	3	2	0	1	5	2	6
Colombia	3	1	0	2	5	3	3
Tunisia	3	0	1	2	5	4	1

England	2	Tunisia	0
Romania	1	Colombia	0
Colombia	1	Tunisia	0
Romania	2	England	1
Romania	1	Tunisia	1
Colombia	0	England	2

GROUP H

	P	W	D	L	F	A	Pts
Argentina	3	3	0	0	7	0	9
Croatia	3	2	0	1	4	2	6
Jamaica	3	1	0	2	3	9	3
Japan	3	0	0	3	1	5	0

Argentina	1	Japan	0
Jamaica	1	Croatia	3
Japan	0	Croatia	1
Argentina	5	Jamaica	0
Argentina	1	Croatia	0
Japan	1	Jamaica	2

SECOND ROUND

Italy	1	Norway	0
Brazil	4	Chile	1
France	1	Paraguay	0

(golden goal; after extra time)

Nigeria	1	Denmark	4
Germany	2	Mexico	1
Holland	2	Yugoslavia	1
Romania	0	Croatia	1
Argentina	2	England	2

(Argentina 4-3 on pens after extra time)

QUARTER-FINALS

Italy	0	France	0

(France 4-3 on pens after extra time)

Brazil	3	Denmark	2
Holland	2	Argentina	1
Germany	0	Croatia	3

SEMI-FINALS

Brazil	1	(Ronaldo 46)
Holland	1	(Kluivert 87)

(Brazil 4-2 on pens after extra time)

France	2	(Thuram 47, 70)
Croatia	1	(Suker 46)

3rd PLACE PLAY-OFF

Holland	1	(Zenden 1)
Croatia	2	(Prosinecki 13, Suker 36)

FINAL

July 12 – Stade St Denis, Paris

Brazil	0	
France	3	(Zidane 27, 45, Petit 90)

Acknowledgments

This book would not have been possible without the help of
Rick Mayston and Matt Stevens

Thanks also to
Steve Torrington, Dave Sheppard, Brian Jackson, Alan Pinnock,
Peter Wright, Trevor Bunting, Simon Taylor, Sheila Harding,
Christine Hoy, Maureen Hill, Anthony Linden, Carol and Cliff Salter,
Matthew Nee, Tom and Harry Nettleton.

Designed by: John Dunne

Pre press by Croxsons

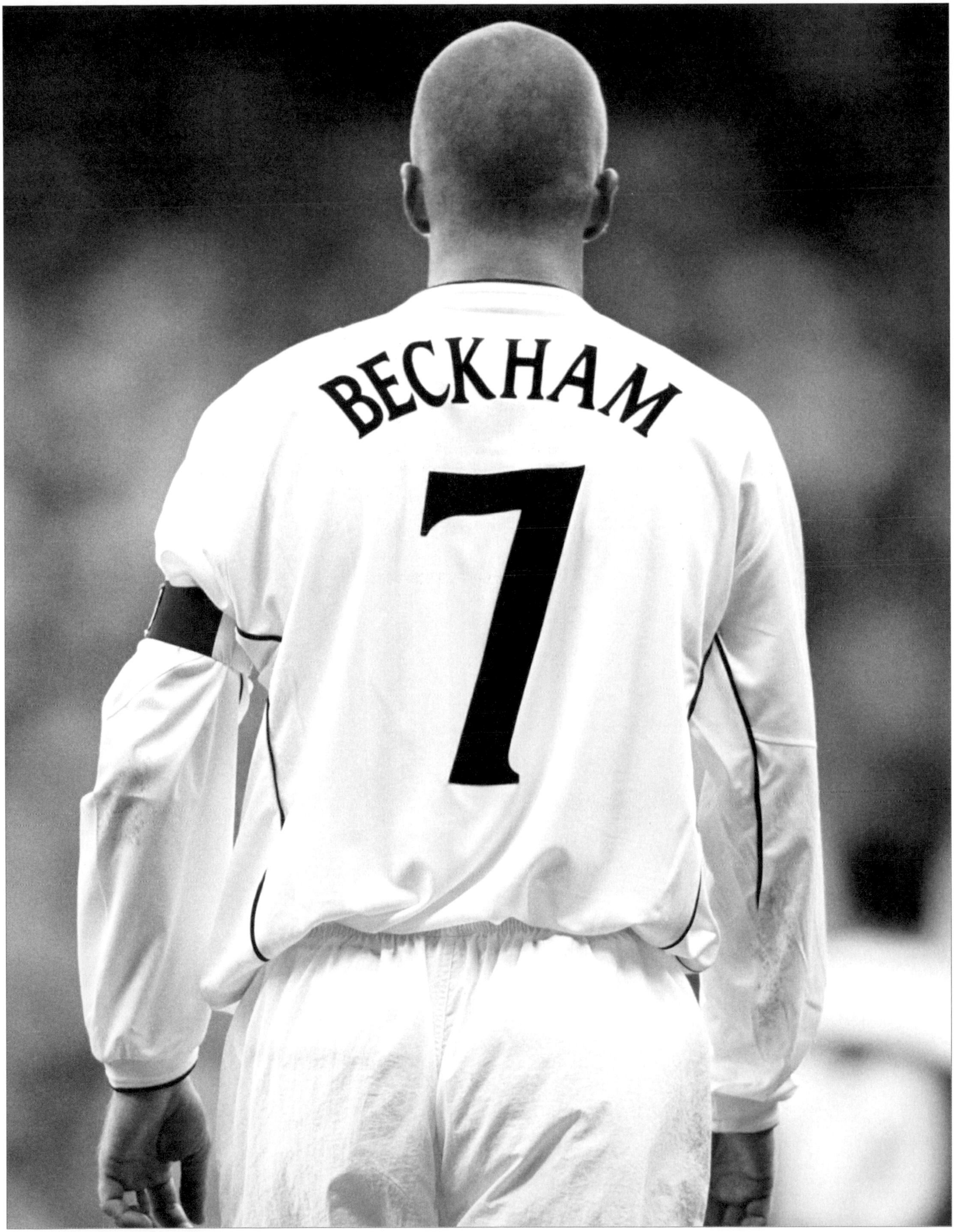
BECKHAM
7